The Secret Life of Dog Catchers

An Animal Control Officers Passion to

Make a Difference

Shirley Zindler

ISBN:9781481839211

For Paul

Note to the Reader

The people, animals and situations in this book are based on my experiences as an animal control officer, animal rescuer, wife and mother. The names and identifying features of many of the characters and events have been altered to maintain the privacy of those involved.

We cannot all do great things. But we can all do small things with great love.
— Mother Theresa

A portion of book sales will be used for animal and children's causes.

Contents

Prologue

I was born to animal-loving parents who took me home from the hospital to a variety of dogs, cats, horses and other animals. There's a photo of me at only a few months of age wearing a little pink dress and apparently all alone on horseback. My dad is concealed from view, standing behind the horse and holding me up. Both grandmothers were horrified thinking I was alone up there, but I love that photo.

Much of my childhood was spent on horseback and in the company of dogs. By the time I was five years old I was riding the range and moving cattle alongside my parents. My sister, Dena, was born when I was six, and soon after that, my parents divorced. Mom, Dena and I moved from the ranch in Oregon to an apartment in California.

It was an adjustment moving to the confines of the apartment. I missed my dad and the animals terribly. A succession of beloved and adored cats, pet rats, parakeets and other small animals followed, but I longed for the horses and dogs. I wasn't complete without a canine buddy to romp with. Unfortunately, however, a horse was out of the question, and dogs weren't allowed in the apartment.

At ten I told my mom I wanted to move in with my dad, who was living in Idaho with my stepmother, Boo, and my half-brother. I loved my family and friends, but I could have a dog at my dad's house, and my need for a dog was overwhelming.

Soon after I made the move, Boo brought home a darling terrier mix puppy I named Shanka. I was in heaven with my buddy following me everywhere and sleeping in my bed at night. It was also wonderful to be able to ride again. I must have explored half of Idaho on horseback with Shanka trotting alongside.

At first I wasn't big enough to lift our heavy western saddles, so I rode bareback. I took a lot of spills but soon developed wonderful balance. I thrilled in looking for wildlife and loved the jackrabbits and ground squirrels that were so abundant there. I had my freedom and never came to any harm.

A year later, my mom had moved to a place I could have my dog and a horse. I returned to California. My first horse there, Pepper, was a beautiful paint gelding. I rode him all over our neighborhood, with Shanka in tow.

When I was fourteen, I helped some neighbor kids train their two-year-old filly, Cali. Cali was friendly but had never been handled. We taught her to lead and lunge, got her used to the saddle, and then I climbed up. After a few tumbles early on, Cali and I became best friends. She became a nice, solid riding horse you could take anywhere.

Besides riding my horses for pleasure, I was also entering horse shows, but Pepper had some recurring lameness so I began riding other people's horses more. I especially enjoyed riding horses with behavior problems and working them through their issues. I was pretty fearless back then and loved working with difficult horses. It was rewarding to see them learn what was expected of them and start to improve.

Around that time, a friend gave me a horse he'd bought at a livestock auction. He had seen a three-year-old untrained Appaloosa/Quarter horse mix gelding and he planned to bid on him. When he stepped out for a moment, the horse passed through the auction and was bought by a slaughterhouse for dog food. My friend offered the guy $50 over what he had paid and gave the horse to me.

"Geronimo" became my new project. He was terrified and his neck was heavily scarred from being roped and probably choked down. But as soon as he trusted me we had a blast. He, too, became a faithful friend and blossomed into an exceptionally gentle and reliable mount. After that, several neighbors asked me to train horses for them and I had a lot of fun and stayed out of trouble that way.

When I was almost sixteen I was at the neighbor's to take Cali out for a ride when I noticed a new guy playing basketball with the teens who lived there. I wasn't very interested in boys, but I thought he was cute. Later that day I was introduced to Paul Zindler. I liked his smile and his green eyes. I was raising some orphaned raccoons on a bottle at home, and Paul asked to see them. We soon became inseparable friends, hiking and riding horses together. One overcast December day I invited Paul to go riding into the hills. We came across some mistletoe and picked some to take home. As we neared the house, Paul asked me to stop. A light mist was falling as we reined in the horses. He held up the mistletoe and leaned across the horses to kiss me. We fell deeply in love, and he remains the love of my life to this day.

My teen years passed without much of the drama that often accompanies that time of life. I spent time with Paul and my friends and was busy with my animals. I showed dogs and horses and a variety of other livestock and I tried to rescue every needy creature I found.

When I was around eighteen I walked into the Rohnert Park animal shelter to see what it was like. Volunteers Carol and Marilyn welcomed me and showed me the animals. One tiny kitten was failing and near death. I asked if I could try to save her and, to my surprise, they agreed. I took "Sugar" home and fed her tiny amounts of warmed formula with a little Karo syrup every hour or so and she started responding. Eventually, she recovered fully and my Uncle Steve's family adopted her.

A lifelong love of shelters was born. I held volunteer and paid positions there and at several other shelters after that. I also worked in a couple of daytime and emergency vet clinics and loved caring for sick and injured animals.

Paul and I married after college. We desperately wanted children and our son Scott was born the following year. Four years later we welcomed our daughter, Nikki. Gazing into the eyes of my babies, I knew, without a doubt, that I was meant to be a mother. I felt like a mama lioness, prepared to fight to the death for her cubs. Those fierce maternal instincts seem to be what keeps me longing to protect and rescue every needy animal and child I come across.

When the kids were little, I continued volunteering at shelters and fostering animals in need. We also took in a foster child, Joseph, who was removed from his biological parents. Scott, Nikki and Joseph (who was later adopted by another family) were surrounded by puppies and kittens, orphaned wildlife and other animals. They watched wide-eyed as an abandoned Rottweiler delivered puppies in our living room and they loved helping bottle-feed baby squirrels and other orphans.

When Nikki started first grade I took a job as a vet tech at our county animal shelter. The people and animals there quickly became my second family, my home away from home. It was challenging, rewarding, and sometimes emotionally devastating.

After several years as a vet tech at the shelter I became an animal control officer for the same department. The freedom of being out in the sunshine (and sometimes the pouring rain) and the endless variety in the field appealed to me. I couldn't ask for a job that suits my personality better. The emergencies feed my adrenaline-junkie side. The rescues nurture my need to rush out and save the world. The orphaned and broken satisfy my overdose of maternal hormones. Of course, facing off angry gang members or getting called out at 2:00 a.m. aren't my favorite things, but it's all part of the job. I'm doing what I've always done, now I just get paid for it.

Today, our busy household consists of three adults — me, Paul, and our dear friend Mickey, a sort of beloved live-in Grandma to all. There are three kids: teenaged son, Scott, teenage daughter, Nikki, and preteen niece, Shay. We also have our share of furry couch warmers. The dogs are Rocky, Katie, Luci, and Hula. Rocky is an older Pug/Chihuahua mix who was rescued from a busy highway by some friends many years ago. Katie is an elderly Borzoi, who is regal and sedate and the last of my show dogs. Luci, the Doberman, is a once-stray shelter dog whose background we know nothing about. She was a wild and unruly adolescent who, with training and exercise, has become my constant companion. The baby of the family is Hula, a beautiful Golden Retriever who gets into constant trouble but is endlessly patient and tolerant of the foster animals that come through. The cats are Jesse, who came to the shelter as a sickly feral kitten some time ago, and Chuck, also a formerly feral kitten who had been hit by a car and brought to us by a neighbor. They rule the household with the sense of entitlement typical of cats. A couple of horses, Joe and Roanie, and some chickens round out the family.

Over the years, our family has included hundreds of fosters, needy creatures that stayed for days, weeks or months. There have been dogs and puppies, cats and kittens, raccoons, skunks, squirrels, newborn calves and lambs. We've had puppies and kittens born in our living room and we've bottle-fed raccoons in the kitchen. We've even raised skunks on the back porch.

Come along and share my life for a while.

1. The Flood

The muddy, rapidly rising water swirled and eddied around the small sandbar where the old dog lay. She appeared to be an elderly Lab mix and her faded coat was sodden and dirty. The white face sagged into the wet ground and she seemed to have given up. Who knows how long she struggled before pulling herself onto this tiny island in the center of the rushing torrent.

It was New Year's Day and the animal shelter was closed. I was the on-call officer for emergencies. This situation certainly fit the definition, as the dog didn't look like she could last much longer. Rain was falling hard, with flooding that had started the day before. This old girl must have been swept in. The creek ran behind a small, rural town, and a resident had spotted her and made the call.

I started down the embankment toward her, but slipped and began sliding toward the water. I landed on my rear, gasping as the cold and wet seeped through my uniform to my skin, but managed to grab some exposed roots and stop my descent. I scrambled back up, wiping my muddy hands on my uniform pants, and I surveyed the area in dismay. The bank was steep, the water too fast to swim and the sandbar was at least fifteen feet out. None of my equipment would reach that far. I usually love the challenge of coming up with a solution to the wide range of difficulties that we encounter, but I was starting to feel desperate as the rain came down and the old dog lay almost lifeless. Only the methodical rise and fall of the chest showed there was still hope.

I toyed briefly with the idea of roping her and dragging her through the water but her head was down and even if I could manage to throw a rope around her there was a good chance of choking or drowning her when I pulled her through the fast-moving water. If only I had a long board or something I could lay over the water and walk or crawl to her on. A ladder seemed the best option I could think of, but where to get one? I glanced around as I brainstormed, and there it was: a fire station a block away.

I ran through puddles and banged on the station door, hoping I wasn't too late. A group of firefighters sat at a table playing cards, and they looked up in surprise at the soggy, muddy blonde on the step.

Within minutes a fire truck pulled up at the creek. Four firefighters in full gear climbed out and lowered a long ladder down to the sandbar. The moment it touched the earth, I started to climb down the ladder, but the firefighters politely shooed me out of the way. I watched the dog look up briefly but barely move as two burly men smoothly and gently lifted her onto a canvas stretcher. It was a thrill to see her carried to safety.

We wrapped the exhausted dog in blankets and settled her on a thick comforter in the enclosed back of my truck. I took a moment to stroke her wet face and she gave my hand the briefest lick before closing her eyes. I saw the look of longtime neglect about her. A deep, stained groove in the fur around her neck suggested a lifetime on a chain and her long nails were curled and growing back into the pads of her feet. I checked her gums for shock. They were pale, not the healthy pink I like to see, but not as ghost white as would be expected if she were critically ill. Her teeth were worn clear down in the front, which happens when dogs chew at themselves because of fleas. Indeed, as I looked into her face, I could see the fleas crawling, frantic to avoid the soaking wet skin. This poor girl's had a rough life, I thought miserably. Nobody's going to claim her.

I've seen it a million times. She gave a deep sigh as I shut the double doors.

Before I could finish thanking my helpers, my pager sounded again. The emergency response team asked me to head for the Red Cross Shelter at the high school where people who had been evacuated from flooded areas needed assistance with their pets. The Animal Shelters Mobile Animal Clinic had been brought in to take in pets from people who were flooded out and had no place for their animals. One of our shelter vets was volunteering at the clinic doing intakes and exams on the animals, so that was a perfect place to head with the dog. When we arrived, the dog was examined and placed in a warm kennel. A couple of volunteers hovered around, showering her with TLC. Vivacious women with graying hair and generous smiles, they looked like people you could count on.

It was time to move on. The vet wanted to observe the dog for a while in the clinic and there were multiple animals that needed transport to the shelter for safekeeping until their owners could claim them. I loaded up a chow chow, a black Lab, a pit bull and several cats and headed for the shelter. As I drove, my pager went off again and again. I did my best to field the calls and quickly made my charges comfortable at the shelter before heading back out.

I normally love driving around our beautiful county north of San Francisco, but I barely noticed the rolling hills, oaks and vineyards as I hurried from call to call. It was impossible to handle all the emergencies that came in about animals affected by the flood though I rushed from call to call that entire day. I was haunted by the ones I couldn't reach and tried to remember my motto, which is critical in this job: just do the best you can do, that's all you can do.

In spite of how busy I was, my thoughts kept drifting back to the old dog as I drove. Could I take her home and foster her, then find her a home? I already had a full house with my own animals and other dogs I was fostering. And even if I took her temporarily, who was going to adopt an elderly, neglected dog? It's a constant dilemma for animal control officers and shelter workers. We can't save them all, and it's easy to burn out and get discouraged. The secret is to focus on the good we do, but sometimes that's easier said than done.

14

Late in the day I made another run to the mobile clinic to pick up more refugee pets. The same two volunteers sat with the old dog, who slept on a blanket between them. She had received a warm bath and blow dry and her nails were trimmed to a comfortable length. She looked loved. I asked how she was doing. "Oh, much better," one of the volunteers responded eagerly. "She ate some food and we've named her Sara. If no one claims her we're going to adopt her."

I felt a wave of gratitude and relief wash over me as I looked at them. I could see these were caring people who would surround this old girl with love for her final years. The flood may have been a tragedy to many, but for one old dog it was the start of a new life.

2. A Day in the Life

"I could never do your job. I love animals too much," people say. "I would just cry all the time!"

Shelter workers and animal control officers hear these words all too often. I understand the intention, but if you think about it, it's pretty insulting, like we must not care about animals or we couldn't do our jobs. My response, with a smile, is always, "I love animals too much not to." Someone has to do this work and who better than someone who cares enough to do a good job.

Let me give you an example of a fairly typical day, starting when the alarm goes off at 6:00 a.m.

Paul has already left for work and the kids are still sleeping when I get up and let the dogs out, get dressed and rake my long blonde mane into a ponytail. I feed my dogs and horses and my latest foster mama dog and her six pups. I make lunches for the kids and grab a cup of coffee, an apple and a boiled egg. I'm out the door by 6:30 a.m. with Luci, my rescued Doberman, trotting by my side. We get into my truck, and Luci takes her place on the seat beside me.

On the way to work, I pick up the newspaper. I arrive a few minutes early, with time to sip some green tea and scarf down my boiled egg and some wheat toast and peanut butter. I skim the newspaper with Luci settled on her bed under my desk.

Around 7:00 a.m. I log on for my shift and check my email. There are several photos and updates from people who have adopted my former foster dogs or cats. These always make my day. I get some lost pet reports, several shelter updates, a couple of rescue stories and some jokes from coworkers. I quickly respond to the emails that need it and then pull up my calls for the day. I research the addresses of calls that have owner information so I'm aware of any prior history and licensing status.

Next comes a walk through the shelter to check on the animals. Though it's no longer my job and there is a group of dedicated vet techs that take excellent care of the animals, the shelter is still my baby and I like to be involved. I spot a timid terrier mix huddled in the corner of the kennel. She's tan with scruffy hair and looks absolutely terrified. I spend a few minutes coaxing her with the treats that are always in my pocket. She cautiously approaches, tentatively takes a treat from me, and finally climbs in my lap. I cuddle her gently for a few moments and by the time I leave she's wagging her tail. It's amazing how a few minutes can change a dog's attitude.

As I work my way past dogs of all shapes and sizes I'm amazed by the number of wonderful animals in our care. There are some darling pit bull mix puppies and many purebred adult Pits. I see purebreds, including German shepherds, a boxer, a beagle, poodles, Chihuahuas, a Cairn terrier, and a black Lab, as well as mixed breeds of all sorts. Most of the dogs are friendly but a couple of them are extremely aggressive. A few are in terrible condition, neglected, mangy, elderly, matted. We have a veterinarian on staff and the animals receive medical treatment as needed. If time allows, we bathe and groom them. Volunteers come in to help as well and do a fantastic job of making life better for the shelter animals.

I talk to the dogs as I pass, offering a kind word and a little encouragement. I spend a few moments in the cat rooms cuddling a variety of beautiful kitties and then visit the small animal areas where some sweet pet rats, rabbits and guinea pigs await adoption. On the way back outside I admire the goat, chickens and a potbellied pig that were picked up as strays.

I've taken longer than I intended to, and I hurry to load my rifle and shotgun into the truck. As I walk past our intake area a group of inmates from the local jail is arriving for their shift working in the kennels. They are a motley group of men who stare as I walk by with my guns, blonde pony tail swinging and Doberman Luci trotting by my side. "Man, don't mess with her," one of them remarks. I smile and say, "All a girl really needs is a shotgun and a Doberman." They laugh at that while I load my guns and then head back inside to grab my list of calls and my duty belt. The belt weighs a ton but carries critical equipment, including a collapsible asp, a can of pepper spray, a portable radio, handcuffs, a pocket knife, a flashlight and ammunition.

Luci settles in the passenger seat while the truck warms up and I review my list of calls and decide what order to do them in, according to priority and location. One of the clerks approaches me as I am about to leave.

"Shirley, hang on a minute. I've got a call of a skunk in a swimming pool for you." She gives me the information and I thank her and head there first. Rescues are my favorite calls; I just hope I'm not too late.

When I pull up at the call I notify dispatch of my arrival by radio and then approach the house. A sweet-faced older woman greets me at the door with a sigh. "Oh, my goodness, I'm so glad you're here," she says, her white curls bobbing as she leads me around to the back of the house with careful steps. She plucks at my sleeve and points to the pool with a trembling finger.

The skunk is a youngster and he's clinging desperately to the hose that attaches to the pool cleaner. It's all that has saved his life. He has probably been there for many hours and is exhausted. Glancing around the yard I see a rake leaning against a tool shed. I scooped the little guy out and he's so tired and relieved to be on dry ground he doesn't show the slightest interest in spraying me and ambles off toward the shrubbery. My caller is ecstatic. She thanks me profusely and I leave with a feeling of satisfaction. The day is off to a good start.

Back in the truck, I check my dispatch printout. My next call is a complaint of a couple of German shepherd mixes that are allowed to run loose and cause trouble in the neighborhood. I head for the dog owner's home and am not surprised to see the dogs playing in the street when I arrive. They're friendly and run up to greet me, then follow me to the door as I contact the owner. The cheerful young brunette explains that it really isn't her fault since the dogs keep digging under the fence. She leads me around the corner of her house and points to the hole under the fence. The dogs too, romp eagerly over to the hole and inspect their accomplishment before bouncing back to me and jumping around with obvious enjoyment.

I tell her she is responsible for her dogs' actions and give her some tips on improving her fence as well as on training and providing exercise for the two frisky young animals. The dogs are not licensed, so I inform her that I'm not going to write her an at-large citation this time, saving her a significant fine, but I am going to give her a fix-it ticket for licensing. Like most people, she is grateful to avoid the fines and doesn't complain about the license cite. It's a diplomatic way to do our job and still come out the good guy. When I finish up, the dog owner thanks me and promises to work on the fence as I wave good-bye.

Next, I head out to pick up a found dog someone is holding at their home. A bearded man with a big smile shows me to his garage where he has confined the dog, a goofy adolescent male pit bull. He's a shiny brindle, rippling with muscle, and he wiggles himself almost to pieces when I slip the lead on him. The finder explains that he was walking his own Golden Retriever on a nearby trail when the Pit came bouncing along, thrilled to find a friend. The dog followed them home, where this nice gentleman had confined him to keep him safe from the nearby busy road. I lift the probably 70-pound dog into the truck and thank the man for his help.

I'm starting to head across town to my next call when dispatch pulls me up on the radio.

"514, Sonoma 5."

"514" is my call sign and "Sonoma 5" is dispatch. I quickly respond. "Go ahead, Sonoma 5."

"I have an injured cat call. Can you copy?"

Our dispatcher, Leslie, gives me the information on a cat that has been hit by a car. It's several miles away, but I maneuver through traffic as quickly as possible and reach the unfortunate kitty within minutes. A distraught passerby is directing traffic around a fluffy black and white cat lying flat-out and breathing hard on the blacktop. I kneel next to the animal, making a hurried assessment as I do a lightning-quick microchip scan and carefully scoop the animal into a well-padded carrier. There wasn't a microchip, so I put the cage in the truck and head directly to the shelter, where I rush the cat into the treatment room.

The vet techs drop their tasks and begin work on my patient while the vet finishes the spay surgery he's working on. I give the staff a brief history on the cat, take a photo and enter the information into the computer. The photo will be posted online almost immediately, giving the owner a chance to locate their pet by computer. I then vaccinate, photograph and kennel the brindle pit bull and head back out.

While I was at the shelter a call came in for loose goats, so I again detour from my scheduled calls and head for the area where they are reported to be. The five goats are grazing contentedly alongside the road and I can see the sagging fence nearby that is their likely route of escape. Sure enough, when I get out of the truck and approach them they run toward the downed area and leap over. I pull the wire tight and twist it to keep it intact temporarily and then head for the nearby home.

An older Hispanic man answers my knock, but he doesn't speak English, so I attempt to communicate in my very limited Spanish. Luckily, I seem to be getting the point across and he nods, looking out at the goats. His brown, lined face breaks into an understanding smile as I pantomime chasing them back inside and that he needs to repair the fence. I give him a written warning, which I hope someone he knows will translate for him, and return his smile.

20

At last I have a minute to catch up and head home for my half-hour lunch break. I let Luci out of the truck and greet my other dogs and hurry to let my foster dog and her pups out to play, then scoop the kennel and top off their water bowls. The pups are seven-week-old mixed breeds. They're adorable, but they're big, hairy, four-legged eating and pooping machines and their care is never-ending. As much as I love all my fosters and miss them when they go, there is still a sense of relief when they leave for their new homes at eight weeks of age. Of course, there is always another foster waiting, so as soon one dog or litter goes to a new home, another takes their place. I always have extra dogs or cats at home.

Where do all of these animals stay? Throughout my property are several spacious kennels with cozy doghouse s and hammock-style beds. One of the kennels is attached to a shed with electricity for heat when needed, and a kennel in the garage has a dog door to a private yard. Small dogs with litters of pups are usually kept in the house, but because I'm away at work all day the outdoor pens are a good setup for the larger dogs. When I'm home the dogs get the run of a fenced half-acre orchard area and they love getting out to explore. They can socialize with my dogs, and company frequently comes and plays with them. I keep lots of toys available, including milk cartons and cardboard boxes for them to play with.

As I finish my break, I mix up the puppies' kibble and call them back into the kennel for a cuddle and a meal. As they chow down I glance at my watch and realize my time is up, so Luci and I head out to the truck and get back on the road. Driving away, it occurs to me I never did eat lunch. I carry snacks in the truck to compensate for irregular breaks and I nibble some trail mix and an apple as I drive.

I call in on the radio, and dispatch gives me a call of an injured deer on a rural road some distance away. I delay my other calls and head that direction. I drive up and down for some time with vague directions until I finally see the unfortunate doe lying in a ditch off the side of the road. Sadly, she has a broken leg and other serious injuries and is unable to rise. Having volunteered with wildlife rescue for many years I know that adult deer are nearly impossible to rehabilitate when injured or sick. They are so reactive to any kind of interference they tend to injure themselves more thrashing around in their panic, which also puts the rescuer at risk. It breaks my heart, but leaving her to suffer is unthinkable. I release my gun lock and load my rifle, then sight down the barrel and pull the trigger. I turn away for a few moments, breathing in the fresh air, studying the view across the meadow. The doe is still and quiet when I look back, no heartbeat, no eye reflex. I load her up in the truck and drive to the nearby wildlife rescue facility. They will feed the meat to the mountain lions, coyotes and other carnivores housed at the rescue center.

The next call is about a skinny horse. When I arrive at the location, I spot a ribby mare in the front pasture. A woman, presumably the owner, comes stomping out of the house. "Oh, what the hell do you want?" she gripes. "Why don't people mind their own damn business? There's nothing wrong with my horse."

She's a sour-faced woman with limp, bleached-blonde hair, a baggy, shapeless sweatsuit and a cigarette. I do my best to put her at ease with a smile and let her know we just need to check on the welfare of her horse. She waves her cigarette around and starts into full cry again as we walk toward the overgrazed pasture. "She's eighteen years old for heaven's sake, of course she's thin, what do people expect. Why the hell do people want to cause trouble! I ought to just put her to sleep."

I try to tune her out as I prepare to examine the mare. The swaybacked sorrel with a blaze approaches us eagerly. She's definitely too thin, with hips and ribs easily visible, but otherwise she appears healthy, eyes bright, moving okay. Her feet haven't been cared for but they have chipped off to an acceptable length. Eighteen really isn't very old for a horse, and I ask about her feeding schedule and veterinary care.

"She gets hay every day, what the hell else does she need? I've had horses all my life; I don't need you telling how to take care of my horse." Her eyes flash as she dares me to do something about it.

"When is the last time she was seen by a vet?" I ask.

"I do my own vet care. Maybe I should just shoot her. Would that make you happy?"

"Horses should have a yearly exam and most need their teeth floated every year or two," I say, doing my best to ignore her cutting remark. People love to guilt-trip us by threatening to kill their animals and trying to make it our fault, and I wasn't buying it. She gives me a steely-eyed stare and, between clenched teeth, says, "She's fine!"

In the barn, I find the hay is very poor quality. The mare would probably gain weight if she were wormed and fed some quality hay and grain, but the woman is being so difficult I doubt she'll take my recommendation. If she were willing to work with me I'd probably give her a few weeks to try increasing the feed and see how the horse does, but since I can't even communicate with this woman, I decide maybe she will listen to the vet.

"Ma'am, I'm sorry but your horse needs to be seen by a vet. I will give you two weeks to have a vet out and you will need to follow the vet's recommendations for care and feeding."

She glares daggers at me and starts swearing again, so I make sure I can see her out of the corner of my eye as I write her a written warning to have the horse seen by a vet. As I climb into the truck, the woman continues to hurl abuse at me. "Get the hell off my property! Why don't you go catch a dog or something? You don't know *Jack shit*!"

After a few minutes of stroking Luci's sweet face, my blood pressure returns to normal. I'm caught up on my calls, so I drive around, patrolling some of our problem areas for strays. I pull into a nearby park for a break and use my cell phone to return some phone calls from people interested in my foster pups. I interview them at length to see if they are a good match for the babies I've cared for the last several months. When I hang up, a gentleman walks up to my driver's window and asks me a few questions about dealing with his neighbors' barking dogs. I give him some information and he continues on his way. All is quiet. I can tell by the lack of radio traffic that my coworkers are caught up as well.

When the radio crackles to life again, there's a request to pick up a litter of kittens found near a creek. We don't normally pick up cats unless they are sick or injured, but these are babies and the finder has no transportation so I head to his location. The young man who made the call about the kittens is homeless, with a face that speaks of hard luck and bad choices, and he's worried to death about the kittens, which he found in the brush near where he had been sleeping. The three babies appear to be about four weeks old and are feral. They flatten their little ears and hiss and spit at me as I approach. At this age they will tame down in no time, but I still find it amusing that they are so tiny and yet put on such a ferocious display. I try to imagine what animal would want to eat them but reconsider the possibility after that terrifying exhibition of ferocity.

I scoop up the babies and place them in carrier with a soft blanket, while reassuring the young man that we will take care of them. Back at the shelter I am relieved to find we have a foster home available for them. If not, I would have taken them, but I already have the litter of pups fostered at home and I have enough to do.

After completing the kittens' impounds and settling them in to await pickup by the foster family, I check on my hit-by-car cat from that morning. He's resting comfortably in the shelter hospital and it appears he will survive. I sit down at my desk, Luci curls up on her bed underneath it, and I attempt to complete my endless paperwork. It's nearly the end of my ten-hour shift but I'm on call tonight, so who knows when I'll get home. Our officers rotate all-night on-call shifts for emergencies, with the police and sheriff's departments dispatching to us after hours. Some days I leave for work before any of my family is up and get home after they are in bed. Paul and the kids have learned to manage without me when I get called out, but it's still a challenge to balance everything as my family is so important to me.

I'm not even halfway through my paperwork when I get another call. I put Luci in the truck again, jump into the driver's seat, and head out. This time it's a report of an aggressive dog charging at people. It's the mean part of town, a dicey neighborhood, and I'm on alert as I approach the dog's location. Sure enough, a big black Rottweiler comes roaring out from behind a graffiti-covered fence as I arrive. Hackles up and growling, he stops and stands rigid, staring me down coldly as I reach for my catch pole. I try happy talk and toss him a cookie. That sometimes does the trick, but not today.

Luci watches anxiously from the truck as I approach the dog slowly, wishing for some back up in case he attacks me. I see a crowd of shady young men watching from a distance, but I doubt they'll help if I get into trouble. They would probably like to see me get mauled. This neighborhood is generally anti–law enforcement of any kind. I realize I should probably call the sheriff's department, but I already have the dog cornered near the fence, so I cautiously continue.

Eyes blazing, teeth bared — a very intimidating sight indeed — his growling increases in volume as I get closer. One wrong move and he's going to blow, either to escape or attack. In almost every case the dog will chose escape when confronted in this way, but it's still an extremely vulnerable position to be in as I need both hands on the catch pole. If he comes for me and I miss with the pole there won't be time to reach for anything else to protect myself. This must be what a bomb technician feels like, I think, as I slowly close in.

With a sigh of relief I lower the noose over the dog's snarling face and tighten it to a safe level. "Let's go buddy," I say, as the dog finally submits and follows me to the truck.

Like most aggressive dogs, his behavior is fear-based. He's saying, "You're scaring me so I'll act ferocious to make you go away." Once he had no other choice and I hadn't harmed him, he came along fairly peacefully and I got him into the truck without incident, then shut and locked the dog-box door.

I practically leap into the truck, ready to leave this scary neighborhood while my gang-banger audience watches, but as I start to pull out, a beat-up black Camaro screeches around the corner and shudders to a stop in front of my truck, partly blocking my escape. A furious young man jumps out and practically climbs in my window. He's yelling into my face. "Where's my dog?

I want my dog! WHERE IS MY FUCKING DOG?" His face is contorted with rage and I'm getting a nightmare close-up of the tattoos on his neck, some of them even creeping up his shaved scalp. Luci stands rigidly, on alert on the seat beside me. She's been taught to stay quiet in a variety of situations, but I know she'll intervene if he touches me and I don't want her hurt. I try to keep my voice calm as I finger the pepper spray on my belt. "Sir, what does your dog look like?"

"He's a Rottweiler and I know you have him 'cause my homies called me!" He practically spits the words into my face and Luci starts to growl low in her throat. He backs off somewhat at that, and it's comforting having her there, but I'm at the ready with my foot tapping the gas in case I need to floor it. If I hit his car, well, too bad.

"How did your dog get out?" I ask quietly, trying to calm him down.

"Somebody left the gate open," he grumbles.

Is it my imagination or is he a little less hostile?

"He's a beautiful dog," I say, with a smile. "I'd hate to see him get hit by a car out here."

"Yeah, he was my brother's dog. My brother was capped right in front of my house last year."

His voice is quieter and I hear the pain in his words. Luci's posture eases. "I'll tell you what," I say. "How about if I waive the citation and fine for your dog being at large. That will save you a few hundred dollars. But I have to write you a fix-it ticket for licensing and neutering."

"Nah, man, he's licensed and neutered," the young man says.

I call in to the shelter and give them his information, and to my surprise, they show a currently licensed and neutered dog. I even peek into the truck to make sure, and it's true, a glance between the dogs rear legs reveals that the dog is neutered. The wonders of this job never cease to amaze me.

I think about the situation for a moment. The dog really hasn't done anything. No one was hurt or even had to take defensive action against the dog. I open the truck and release the dog to his owner with a verbal warning. The young man's face lights up as the dog leaps joyfully into his arms. The mask of ferocity has momentarily slipped and it's just a kid and his dog. He even thanks me. "You're all right, lady."

I drive away with conflicting emotions battling inside of me. I know I could have been in serious danger from either the dog or the man. Either of them could injure, even kill, someone. But we had a positive outcome. I am struck by the similarities in the dog and the young man's expressions when they felt threatened. Yet both showed vulnerability, and both were fairly receptive to kindness and improved with careful handling. This is certainly not a job for anyone who doesn't enjoy working with people as well as animals.

It's past 6:00 p.m. by now, so I head for home instead of the shelter. Luci and I walk through the door and I'm greeted by the aroma of Paul's delicious spaghetti and a big smile and smooch from him. I feel my tension start to ease. Having a supportive home life really helps me survive the ups and downs of this job. Scott and Nikki, both teenagers, aren't overly demonstrative, but they look up from their homework and ask about my day. My niece, Shay, gives me a hug and the dogs crowd around to examine my clothes, fascinated by the smells of my job. I run out and feed the animals while the kids set the table, and when I am done we all sit down to dinner.

Later, I help Shay with homework and then run a hot bath and sink blissfully into it. Paul comes in to visit with me, sitting on the edge of the tub. We talk about our day and the kids, simple stuff, but so enjoyable. He travels a lot as a pilot, and it's good to have him home. We always grab every available moment to spend together.

After my bath, I kiss the kids goodnight and glance at our spoiled rotten dogs and cats slumbering in a variety of cushy beds throughout the house. Thank goodness you guys have no idea, I think, as I see them sacked out. Actually, most of them were rescued from not so great situations, so they do have an idea.

Paul and I climb into bed and hold each other, grateful to be together. We finally doze off at around 10:30.

At 10:45, the phone rings. I pick up the receiver to hear a woman's frantic voice reaching an advanced level of hysteria. There is an opossum in her house, the woman tells me, lured through her cat door by the scent of cat food, and now it's under her bed.

Wildlife in houses is a common situation and each species responds best to a different method. Opossums are quiet and slow and they might show their teeth, but they're pretty easy to handle.

When I finally get the woman calm enough to hear me, I advise her to close all the doors in her house except the one to the outside. I tell her to get a broom and gently sweep the wayward creature toward the open door. I remind her the opossum may keel over and play dead, but she should keep carefully pushing it along until it's outside.

The woman is much calmer now that she knows what to do. A few moments later she comes back on the line to report that, as I'd predicted, the animal decided it would be better off back in the woods.

Grateful I was able to solve the problem over the phone, I hang up and flop back on my pillow. Paul is used to my late-night phone calls and is sleeping peacefully. I doze off, hoping that call will be the only one tonight.

Another day in the life of an animal control officer has come to an end.

3. Attack of the Killer Pugs

I blinked sleepily at the clock on my nightstand as I reached for the phone. It was 12:05 a.m. and I immediately wished I wasn't on call, but the endless ringing of my cell phone could not be denied. The police dispatcher on the other end of the line advised me that a man had been attacked by three dogs and needed an immediate response. I quickly dialed his number.

The man was very upset as he described being out for a peaceful moonlit walk on Skywing Drive. All of a sudden three dogs had charged out of the gloom snarling and growling and trying to attack him. He explained the only reason he wasn't injured was that he had been able to fight the beasts off with some well-executed karate moves. He had seen the animals run back to a nearby home and was adamant that I respond immediately.

Skywing Drive is located in a very elite neighborhood and is not the kind of place you often find out-of-control killer dogs. Further questioning, in fact, revealed the dogs were pugs.

Still groggy with sleep, I shook my head. I must have misunderstood. In my experience, pugs are among the most delightful creatures on the planet. Exceedingly good natured, they usually welcome everyone with wagging tails and laughing mouths. It is almost impossible not to smile at the sight of their buggy eyes and happy, wrinkly, squished-in faces. And they rarely weigh much more than twenty pounds.

But no, he insisted, these were terrifyingly aggressive pugs and I had better hurry before someone less prepared than he wander along unwittingly and be maimed.

I mulled about it all the way to Skywing Drive. There certainly can be nasty dogs of any breed, I reasoned. Sometimes dogs surprise me and, truly, anything is possible in this business.

I pulled up to a gracious home on a beautiful tree-lined street. It's always best to be prepared, but I couldn't quite bring myself to grab a catch pole. I was willing to risk scarred up ankles if that was going to be case.

All was dark and quiet as I walked up the elegant front path lit by the dim glow of a nearby streetlamp. As I approached the entrance, I noticed the front door ajar. Suddenly, three furry bodies rocketed out of the door and down the steps toward me. Loud snuffing and snorting sounds filled the night air as I was surrounded by wild and unruly Pugs. The dogs were ecstatic to find a new friend at this odd hour. They leapt over each other in a frantic attempt to get at me, jumping and clawing at my pants. I could see their sparkly pink jeweled collars glitter as their pink tongues lapped at my knees. Certainly, their greeting could be considered a little overwhelming to someone who wasn't used to dogs.

The dogs escorted me up the steps and panted happily as I rang the doorbell. I was on hyper-alert just in case there was some ominous reason for the door being open at nearly 1:00 a.m., but I didn't see any sign of foul play.

The bleary-eyed, middle-aged owner came to the door, understandably surprised to see me. She looked in shock from me to her dogs and back again as I explained the reason for my call. She chuckled nervously, tightening her plush white bathrobe around her waist. "I must not have pulled the door shut tight after I came in late from bunko."

The Pugs all had current licenses, so I gave her a verbal warning to contain her ferocious pets and bid her goodnight. I really should have issued a written warning since the caller felt threatened, but I couldn't see him going to court and telling the judge he was assaulted by Pugs named Precious, Pansy and Lily.

It's hard to imagine being afraid of those adorable animals, but I try not to be too judgmental. Some people are just not comfortable with dogs. Most people would have recognized they meant no harm, but I could see how their overeager charge in the dark could have startled an unsuspecting person. To the untrained ear, those classic Pug snorts could sound like fearsome growls.

And there were those unusual times, too, like several months earlier when I assisted another officer on a call for two aggressive Pekingese. Pekes can be one-family dogs and some don't appreciate strangers. Their small bodies and silky coats combined with sweet squished-in faces made an adorable package, but these two little dogs really did mean business. They had apparently slipped under the garage door as the owners were pulling out one evening. The door closed behind them and the two pampered boys found themselves alone out front. Uneasy, they hung around on the front lawn and every time someone walked by they charged ferociously. Insecure and unaccustomed to being outside among strangers, they quickly saw their ferocious act made people go away, which was the whole point. A neighbor had called animal control, and my fellow officer, Dave Birch, had attempted to corral the little terrors, but he was unable to capture them by himself and the gate was locked so he couldn't just let them back into their yard. They ran under cars and into the street to avoid him. He called me for backup after 20 minutes of futile effort.

When I arrived we were able to corner the Pekes on the porch and slip leads past their snapping mouths and around their thick little necks. I had to entirely wrap each one in a blanket to lift them into the truck so they wouldn't bite me. (I couldn't exactly wrap their short little muzzles like a regular dog.) They would stay at the shelter for safekeeping until the owners could claim them. By the time we reached the shelter they had calmed down and sullenly accepted handling while waiting to be picked up by their grateful owners.

4. Down the Drain

I don't usually start my morning sitting six feet down at the bottom of a storm drain smelling faintly of canned mackerel. Still, it wasn't so bad. It was nice and dry down there at the moment. I had a blanket to sit on and a good book to read. There was something almost peaceful about my place below the sidewalk. Now and then I gazed up from my book through the open manhole to the circle of dappled morning sunlight filtering through a spreading oak overhead. Birds were twittering, my book was engaging, and it was relatively relaxing compared to the often hectic mornings at work.

I paused to shine my light down one of the four long, dark tunnels, which branched off from the small rectangular space where I sat. Far down the pipe, a pair of eyes was barely visible. I pushed the can of cat food closer and called and coaxed, but no luck.

My plan was to wait as long as needed for the frightened kitten to come to me. I had been there nearly an hour already. I knew from the neighbors that the grey kitten had been there since the previous day when someone had dumped a box with mama and babies in this quiet, attractive neighborhood. Some kind neighbors had gathered up the rest of the little family and taken them to a nearby vet clinic, but this little guy had scurried away down the drain before they could get him.

The pipe where the kitten sat was too small for me to fit into. I had tried lowering a trap baited with canned food into the hole and walking through the berry bushes to the far end of the pipe, but the kitten was still out of reach. I was running out of options.

Just as I settled back to my book, I heard a kitten mewing, but the sound was coming from a different direction. I stood, puzzled, and stretched on tiptoe to see out of my hole. Eye level to the sidewalk, I finally isolated the sound. It was coming from a nearby home. I heaved myself up out of the drain and started toward the home.

The resident, dressed in a flowered robe and slippers, came out and began looking around as well.

"It sounds like it's coming from under your porch," I called.

"Oh my! I'm so glad you're here," she called back. "The poor thing has been crying all night but I can't seem to find it."

Together we poked around until I located a tiny gap under the porch. I shined my light in to see a replica of the other kitten peering back at me. I ran back to my truck and got another tin of canned food. This little one wasn't as shy as her sibling and when she smelled the food she scrambled out in an instant. She purred ecstatically as she dug into the food and I stroked her soft fur.

After a minute or two, I carried the kitten back to the truck and set her and her meal on a towel in a small crate. Then, using a rope, I lowered her, still eating, into the storm drain. I was hopeful that the sight of a sibling would be enough to bring the reluctant kitten out of the pipe. There wasn't much room for both me and the cage in the space below, so I watched from above. As I'd hoped, when she finished her meal the kitten began to meow loudly. After a few moments I saw the bright eyes of her sibling peer cautiously from the pipe. He still wasn't in reach, so I climbed back into the hole only to see him again scurry down the pipe.

Meanwhile, the caged kitten mewed and fussed and I wanted to let her out but I was worried about losing them both. As she gazed at me, purring and making biscuits with her furry little paws, I decided to risk it. I picked her up, set the cage up on the sidewalk above me, and settled back on my blanket with the kitten on my lap. In seconds I realized I couldn't have gotten rid of her if I'd wanted too. After her night alone she was desperate for company and she snuggled into my neck, purring contentedly.

I cuddled her close and settled back to my book, grateful that my coworkers were covering my other calls so I could try to wait it out. I was really getting into my book when I became aware of a slight movement in the pipe. The sound of the purring kitten in my arms was reaching the sibling, who looked like he wanted in on some of that good stuff. Maybe the big scary human was starting to look less threatening than being cold, lonely and hungry in the pipe.

Over the next few minutes, the kitten finally eased his way out enough for me to slowly reach over and offer the food. As hungry as he was, he craved company more than food and he crawled onto my lap next to his sister. As I stroked him he began to purr softly, and as he started to feel safe, the sound rose to a crescendo. Both babies purred happily in my arms.

Since the nearby vet clinic had taken the rest of the family, I decided to stop in and check on them. The caring staff immediately offered to take in these two as well and led me to a treatment room where mama and siblings were being kept. They had already been vaccinated and were awaiting spay and neuter surgeries before adoption. The two I brought in joined the group. They closed their eyes, purring blissfully, as mama began to lick them.

5. Lily

One sunny Saturday morning I received a call of an abandoned dog. I arrived at the address to find my caller with a heavily bandaged finger. "Were you bitten?" I asked.

"Well, yes," the woman said, surveying her bandaged finger ruefully. "It was my own fault. I grabbed the poor thing and scared it."

I sighed. Now I had a bite report and quarantine on top of an abandonment case. I entered the dingy mobile home and walked from room to room looking for the dog. The tenants had been evicted and evidence of a rapid departure was everywhere. There was food growing mold on the counters, toys, clothes and garbage scattered around, and an air of poverty about the place. I had forgotten to ask what kind of dog I was looking for, but I could get all the info for my bite report after I captured the offender.

As I opened the door to the last bedroom I was greeted by a shrill high-pitched squeal. The noise belonged to a tiny morsel of a scrawny Chihuahua puppy huddled on a filthy carpet. Most of her hair was missing and she screamed nonstop in terror, not even seeming to take a breath. I approached her slowly and kneeled, holding out a treat, but she continued her assault on my eardrums. When I reached for her, she snapped rapid-fire several times and then leapt away. I tried a few more gentle maneuvers without success and then reached for a tattered towel on the floor. I got her cornered against the wall and wrapped her in the towel, still screaming, biting and fighting with everything she had.

The puppy screamed all the way to the truck, but when I set her inside and closed the door, the noise switched off and was replaced by complete silence. I went back inside, got all the caller's information for the bite report and headed for the shelter.

Most dogs have calmed down and are ready to be friends by the time we get to the shelter. Not this little girl. The screaming started again the second I opened the door to her box. She again tried to bite me. I wrapped her in the towel and took her inside to vaccinate, worm and photograph her. I hated to upset her more, but it was unthinkable to bring her into a shelter without vaccines. I don't think she even noticed the needle her terror at being handled was so great, and she was still so traumatized at the end of the day that I wrapped her in a blanket and took her home with me.

Thankfully, the last of my fostered litter had gone to a new home the day before so I had some time for this little creature I named Lily. It hardly seemed possible that she was a dog, as small and scared as she was. I set her up in a big crate in the living room where she was right in the middle of everything. I put a bowl of tiny pieces of chopped chicken on top of her crate and each time anyone in the family passed by she was given a treat. I also took her out and held her as I worked around the house. After the first few times, she quit trying to bite.

Mickey and the kids were home a lot more than I was and they took her out and played with her while I was at work. Soon Lily was bouncing around underfoot like she owned the place. I introduced her to the other dogs. It was comical to see her nose to nose with the big dogs. Her entire body was not as long as Katie's long Borzoi nose and I had to watch carefully to see that she didn't get stepped on.

As the days passed, her bald patches grew in and her coat started to shine. Her skinny little body filled out and her confidence blossomed. She pranced and played and harassed the cats, who were too haughty to even acknowledge her as she yipped and pawed at them.

When I started bringing Lily to work with me she endeared herself to the entire staff with her delightful ways and silly antics. I interviewed a few people who were interested in her but none seemed quite right. A nice family wanted to adopt her and they had a couple of sweet boys ages eight and ten, but Lily was so tiny and constantly underfoot that I worried about her getting hurt. I steered them toward a sturdy terrier mix that seemed to be a better fit. I also denied a young man who wanted to get her as a surprise birthday gift for his girlfriend. Pets are never good surprise gifts, I told him. I asked him to bring his girlfriend in to meet Lily first. He started arguing and swearing at me at that point, which cinched my decision not to adopt Lily out to him. Finally, a woman came in who had seen Lily's photo on our shelter website and driven several hours to see her. She was a veterinarian who owned a friendly young male Chihuahua. The dogs hit it off instantly. I liked the woman tremendously and was thrilled when she asked to adopt her.

As I watched Lily leave in her new owner's arms, I sniffed a few times and a lump filled my throat. It's so hard to get attached over and over and then to have to say good-bye, but it's also deeply rewarding to see animals adopted into wonderful homes. I headed back inside to finish my paperwork and start another night on call.

6. The Mustang

The wild mustangs huddled together as crowds of spectators gathered around the pens at the Bureau of Land Management auction at the local fairgrounds. Paul and I had come to the auction on my day off to see what it was like. We gazed at the horses for a few moments and then I turned to Paul. "Wouldn't it be fun to train one?" I said.

"Huh?"

"We should adopt one and train it. Wouldn't that be great?" I turned back to watch the wild horses.

Here's where most husbands grab their wives and drag them forcefully away from the premises. Like the SWAT team on a megaphone: "STEP AWAY FROM THE HORSES AND RETURN TO YOUR VEHICLE!" But somehow, by some miracle of fate and luck and God smiling on me, I didn't marry most husbands. Even if Paul had said, "No way, not in a million years, are you out of your skull?" it would have been okay and reasonable. But he didn't. He looked at me, not like he thought it was a great idea or anything, but like he was open to discussion. So…. we discussed it and agreed that I could bid on them if I wanted

39

to. Like the guy just wanted to make me happy and thought, who knows, it probably would be fun.

Bidding opened the next day and I was back early. I walked around, checking my catalog and surveying the horses. I wanted a gelding. It seemed like the geldings I had owned and ridden were more sensible and less moody than the mares. I also wanted a youngster, preferably under a year old but definitely under two. I know from experience that younger animals tame far more easily than older ones. Feral kittens and puppies past eight weeks or so that haven't been handled by people are much less likely to come around well. Granted, some do adjust to one or two people at older ages, but the odds are definitely better the younger they are.

These horses had been born wild and gathered off the range just before the sale. Their only experience with people had been a terrifying roundup following by being forced into trailers and hauled to a holding area where they were run into a chute, branded, vaccinated and vet-checked. A second scary trailer ride took them to the sale. The wild mustangs weren't too fond of humans at that point and adopters had their work cut out for them. Still, I had practically grown up on horses, I had trained some, shown some and ridden endlessly. It seemed challenging but doable.

Right away, I picked out the star of the sale. A golden palomino of about one year old, he had four white socks, a perfect blaze and a thick, wavy, cream-colored mane and tail that contrasted beautifully with his dappled coat. Gorgeous! The bidding was by silent auction, starting at $125. I bid on the palomino a few times but he shot up to $1,350 in no time, way out of my price range. He was the high seller, and I was rather proud of my mustang judging ability.

Besides that palomino, I was outbid on a few more favorites. There were still plenty of young geldings available, but I found myself drawn to a petite buckskin filly. There was nothing remarkable about her, although I have always liked buckskins. Her coat was the color of a deer, a tannish brown with a thick, tangled black mane and tail and there was no white on her at all. Flashy pintos and bays were still available, but I kept coming back to this filly that stood quietly at the back of the pen watching me. I ended the day the proud owner of that three-year-old filly.

I tend to be pretty practical. It's out of character for me to decide I need an 800-pound, totally wild, money-sucking mouth to feed that's never been touched and could kill me with a single kick. I had wanted another horse; either something dead-broke that my husband, kids and non-horsy friends could ride or a project horse. This filly would fall into the category of project horse.

I had seen mustangs in my job. A good percentage of them had been adopted by well-meaning people and ended up as total disasters. In some cases they escaped and no one could get near them or they lived the next twenty to thirty years with no one able to touch them, care for their veterinary needs, or even trim their hooves. But I love a challenge and I knew I'd learn a lot.

The handlers ran my little mustang into a chute, blocked her in and wrestled a halter and long lead rope on her, then ran her into a borrowed stock trailer. At home we backed the trailer up to a paddock attached to our small barn and she bolted out of the trailer into her new home. I tossed some hay into the manger and left her alone for a while to settle in while my two geldings, Joe and Roanie, crowded around the pen inquisitively.

Later, I came back to find the mustang standing in the corner watching me warily. I slowly entered the pen and sat on the ground in the opposite corner. I avoided eye contact and read a book for an hour or so while the filly watched me with her serious big brown eyes.

Normally, I would never leave a halter and lead on a horse as it can be a safety hazard, but with wild mustangs it's recommended the halter be left on for training purposes until the horse is gentled. It also serves to desensitize them to the lead as it touches the horse's legs and body endless times each day as she moves around. When they step on the lead they learn to give their head and they also learn they need to move their feet to release the pressure.

I named the mustang Annie. Each day I set aside time before and after work to hand-feed her. I sat in the pen and gave her all of her hay by hand. She was scruffy and scrawny and I offered grain but, like many mustangs off the range, she wouldn't touch it. I would pour some right on top of her hay and she would use her lips to brush it aside in disgust. She would take hay from me cautiously and I could give the merest brush of my hand to her muzzle but that was it. Any more liberties than that would send her rocketing to the far side of the pen.

After several weeks I reached over and picked up the end of the lead. By now she was accustomed to the lead moving and touching her, but this was something new. She reacted instantly and spectacularly, bolting wildly around the pen as I stayed out of her way and held on. The moment she finally stopped fighting me, I released the lead. I repeated this for the next two days. On the third day Annie stood quietly as I picked up the lead. After a moment I gave a slow, steady tug. I kept up the pressure until she took the tiniest step toward me and then instantly released it. We had our first step. It was only inches, but it was progress.

After that she improved quickly and soon was following me around the pen on a loose lead. I even led her out of the pen, around the fenced pasture and into the round pen for some exercise and grazing, and I could see that she looked forward to her outings. She was so quick and reactive, however, that more than once something startled her and she bolted away from me. The first time it happened I held on to her long lead with all my strength. I didn't want her to learn she could get away. But I was no match for her and the rope sung through my hands as she galloped off in terror, leaving me surveying my burned and bloodied fingers in dismay. The pain was intense and I had to sit down and lean against the barn for a moment, fighting nausea and dizziness. After that I wore leather gloves and she got better all the time.

To my frustration, though, we made almost no progress in the area of touch. I spent several hours in the pen every day after work hand-feeding her, talking to her, cleaning her pen or just sitting quietly on the ground while she snuffled around me, but anything other than a gentle stroke on the muzzle and she would yank away. After a month of this I was discouraged. I dreamed of the day I could comb out her tangled mane, brush her scruffy coat and stroke her. Maybe I really was in over my head. What made me think an animal that had lived totally wild for three years was going to become gentle and trusting?

In the meantime, we continued halter training and started working in the round pen. I spent half an hour in the round pen with her each day, letting her get some exercise and teaching her "walk," "trot," "canter" and "whoa" on the long line. She was incredibly bright and even started following voice commands, but I still couldn't touch her.

I had read about a type of horse training I knew would scare her initially, but I was running out of options and finally decided to go for it. The bamboo-pole method was supposed to be effective with mustangs and other really wild horses. The idea of this method is that you touch the horse with a long light pole in a pen where they cannot get away from it. The horse learns that the pole only goes away when they stop fighting. If it's done right the animal learns that the touching doesn't hurt and is even pleasant. Paul had been following our progress and had spent time with Annie as well and he came to help if I got into trouble.

Paul stood outside Annie's pen as I went in. She was accustomed to my presence now and was usually calm unless I tried to touch her, but the sight of the pole had her on high alert. I stood quietly for a moment and then raised the pole and laid it across her back. She immediately launched straight ahead and crashed against the barn before bolting in a circle around me in a cloud of choking dust. I struggled to keep the end of the pole on her back as she rocketed around the pen, trying frantically to get away from the terrifying thing touching her. After a minute or two of wild circling and crashing around, she froze with her head in the corner, sides heaving and the pole still settled on her back. I removed it right away. "Good girl, Annie, such a good girl, that's my good girl," I crooned to her as I slowly walked out of the pen.

Paul grinned at me while waving the dust away from his face. "People pay good money to see a show like that."

The next day we tried again with similar results, but the third day she

43

stood calmly as I lowered the pole to her back. She didn't even seem distressed about it, so I started rubbing the pole up and down her back without her moving an inch. I worked it up her neck and back toward her tail, watching for signs of distress but saw none. After a few moments of this I stopped, elated. What a smart girl. It had only taken three times for her to learn to be calm for the pole.

Progress was swift after that. The next day I was able to touch her entire body, up and down the legs, belly and rump with the pole. I slowly worked my way up the pole until I was standing right next to her. She had tolerated my being close in before, but not with the touch. I continued to rub her with the pole as I slid my hand closer and closer to her. Soon my hand was scratching her back along with the pole and we moved on to such impossible liberties as stroking her body and raking my fingers through her tangled mane. She relaxed visibly as I continued to scratch at her rough coat and she even seemed to be enjoying it. I grabbed a rubber curry comb and a hairbrush and finally began to work on her matted mane. She stood quietly for another half hour as I gently separated the tangled strands, her eyes half-closed like any old workhorse. I think she was enjoying the attention, and I was elated but didn't want to overdo it, so I finally left her to process the day. I had groomed a wild mustang and earned some of her trust. It was a milestone day for us both.

For a while after that amazing, breakthrough day, Annie would only let me touch her if I had the pole in my hand. If I entered the pen without it she would bolt away. With the pole I could walk right up and pet her. It was like she knew that she couldn't get away from the pole so she didn't even try, and yet her body language was calm. I believe it was because she knew exactly what to expect with the pole.

Next, I taught her to tie. For a horse that's been free all of her life, tying can be a terrifying experience. I had set a huge railroad tie deep in the ground against the barn in her pen and another out where I often groomed the horses. I took the precaution of putting an extra halter over the top of the one she wore. I wanted to make absolutely certain she didn't break free. Some horses will always fight being tied and it's a real problem, especially if they ever manage to

44

pull free.

I attached a sturdy inner tube to the railroad tie to allow a little bit of give when she pulled and I clipped two heavy-duty leads to it. Leading her to the post, I clipped each lead to one of her halters and slowly stepped back. She stood for a moment looking around but then pulled a little. Realizing that she couldn't move freely sent her into a panic and she set back with all she had.

Watching her fight in terror against her constraints, I felt a wave of sorrow and compassion. How sad for a creature of the wild to be confined and shackled in this way! Her eyes bulged and she leaned back until she was almost sitting down. She jumped and yanked and sweat broke out on her skin as she fought, but after a moment she stopped her battle and stood quivering in place, the leads slack. It was painful to watch, but I knew, as hard as it was, her life would be infinitely better in many ways once she adapted to domestic life. The tradeoff of freedom is a far longer life with plenty of food, water, farrier and vet care, and a lack of predators. It was kind of a toss up as far as I could see. Her life is what it is now. We had to make the best of it, and for her to have the best possible care she needed to learn to be a domestic horse.

I approached her gently, stroked her trembling neck and scratched under her mane where she likes it best. Once she was totally calm, I unclipped her and released her. I fed the horses and headed for the house.

7. Where's the Roast?

One day a frustrated gentleman came into the shelter practically in tears. He had a lovely eight-month-old black Lab puppy named Molly with him. She was friendly, spayed and vaccinated. This man had taken good care of Molly but was surrendering her to the shelter. When I asked why he was giving her up he could barely speak.

"From the moment I brought her home," he said, once he had composed himself, "she has chewed up everything she could reach. The kid's toys, our shoes, all of our new lawn furniture. I mean, for God's sake, she even ate the wheels and pull cord off the lawn mower. There was nothing she didn't chew into mulch." He paused, wincing at the bitter memory. "I just bought a brand new motorcycle. I hadn't even ridden it yet because I still had to register it."

This can't be good, I thought, anticipating his next sentence.

"I put it in the garage." Another long pause. "And she destroyed it. She ate every exposed piece of that bike; it looks like it was mauled by a grizzly bear."

I could sympathize with the guy, but I still had to wonder what he was thinking, putting his bike in the garage with a puppy with a known history of chewing up everything she laid eyes on. I led Molly to our intake room for vaccines and a photo and thought back to some of the puppy antics my own dogs engaged in.

Our old Belgian Tervuren, Tess, is long gone, but when she was a puppy she kept chewing up the garden hose and I kept buying the parts to repair it. I used the hose a lot and it was a pain to roll it up and put it completely out of Tess's reach every time. Invariably, I would forget and come outside to pieces of hose all over the yard. She also chewed the cord to the electric mower. I spliced it and was able to fix it, but I contemplated leaving it plugged in just to break her of it once and for all. I decided that was too risky, but I definitely grumbled under my breath as I finished my repair job for the umpteenth time. Tess also grabbed the doormat off the porch every day and dragged it around the yard. I did come up with a solution for that one, though, by booby-trapping the thing. I tied a bag of aluminum cans to a rope that I then attached to the mat and balanced on top of the propped-open screen door. The next time Tess grabbed the mat the bag of cans came crashing down and chased her until she dropped the mat and ran for dear life. She never touched it again.

Hula was a fairly accomplished chewer as a youngster, too. Paul was poking around the garage one day when he called to me, "Have you seen the spray nozzle for the hose?"

"Yes, I have," I called back rather irritably.

"Well, where is it?"

"Hula chewed it up, swallowed it, digested it and crapped it out all over the yard."

"Oh," Paul responded, with his typical good cheer. I looked over at him and his eyes twinkled at me and my heart did a flip flop. What can I say? I'm crazy about the guy. And Hula's a good girl. She just gets into everything. Or should I say, her people aren't very good at putting stuff away.

But some things you can't put away. Paul had dreamed of getting a BMW Z-3 for years, but we really didn't have much money. Paul is normally a frugal and practical guy, he asks for very little, so when he has an occasional request I do what I can to honor it. We skimped and saved, finally found the used car in our price range and bought it. We drove home with the top down, laughing like kids. The next day we were ready for our first real drive and we went into the garage for the car. To my horror, the pristine white paint was covered with huge, muddy cat prints. Our cat Jessie, a Polydactyl with extra toes and giant feet, had tromped through the mud and then walked all over the hood, leaving a huge mess. I covered my mouth and looked at Paul. He calmly pulled the car out, hosed it off and gallantly opened the door for me. "Shall we?" Unbelievable! Where did I find this guy?

Another day, Paul called me at work sounding a bit shattered. "Hula climbed on the Z, chewed up the cover and then took a dump on the roof. She was still standing up there when I found her." His voice was quiet but I could hear his dismay. Why she would do that to his sporty little convertible? I surveyed the scene later and made a pretty good guess. "I think she just climbed up there out of curiosity, chewed the cover for a while because that's just her, and then couldn't figure out how to get down. She had to go so she went."

And then there was the time with the turkey roast. I had gotten off work early and driven an hour and a quarter to the airport to pick up Paul, but his flight was delayed and it was after 11:00 p.m. when we got home. He was ravenous, it was his birthday, and he was home for only one night, so I really wanted it to be special and cooked his favorite foods. I had asked our teenaged daughter to put the roast away after they ate, but there was no sign of it.

"Where's the roast?" I asked, utterly puzzled, as I searched the refrigerator. "I made a big turkey roast for you for your birthday." The pan sat neatly on the counter with a ring of cooked-on juices showing where it had been.

"Maybe the kids ate it," Paul said, looking around absently before reaching for the peanut butter and jelly.

"It was huge, there's no way they ate it all."

I went to Nikki's bedroom and gently woke her to ask what had happened to the roast. She mumbled sleepily that she had forgotten to put it away and didn't know where it was. I wandered back toward the kitchen, still totally stumped. My eyes rested on Hula, our Golden Retriever, sleeping peacefully on her bed in the dining room. Her eyes were closed and she appeared to be the epitome of innocent sweetness. Hula *is* sweet, but she gets into more trouble than all the other dogs combined and the other dogs were sleeping in other parts of the house. Hmmm, I thought, I wonder....

About then, Shay wandered through on her way to the bathroom. Overhearing our conversation, she said, "I heard something in the kitchen after I went to bed, so I got up. Hula had her feet on the counter, but it was dark so I couldn't see what she was doing. I just told her to get out of there and went back to bed." She rubbed her eyes and continued on her way as Paul and I connected eyes in amazement and then turned to look at the thieving dog. "You are sooooo busted!" I exclaimed, staring at her as she opened her eyes and blinked at me, unconcerned, before resuming her slumber. I turned to Paul. "I can't believe she ate a whole roast."

It's not easy to upset Paul, and he just smiled and shrugged apologetically. Hula is, after all, technically his dog.

After getting over my initial annoyance, I went back to my usual living-with-dogs philosophy, which basically says if the human can't remember to put the roast away, how is the dog supposed to remember not to eat it? I constantly hear people complain that their dog chewed up their $200 shoes or some other valuable item and they are so angry at the animal. It amazes me that the human being of supposedly superior intelligence, who knows how much things cost, can't remember to put away valuable things when they have a bored adolescent dog around.

Not long after the roast incident I had a busy day at work, and then kept getting called out on emergencies because I was on standby. I finally dragged my tired butt home, sat down for dinner, and three bites into it was called out again. I drove out to pick up a stray Border Collie that was chasing chickens, took her to the shelter for impound, came home, fed my four dogs and two new fostered litters of pups and climbed in the bathtub for a relaxing soak before bed.

I let out a long sigh as I settled into the warm water, feeling the stress of the day dissolve as I closed my eyes. As I lay there, I became aware of a sound I couldn't identify, a rhythmic clanging, not too loud, coming from the kitchen. I lay there puzzling over it for a moment before it came to me. That rotten Hula! It was the sound of her tags banging against a pot on the stove. I leapt out of the tub in a fury, threw a towel around myself and roared out of the bathroom and around the corner to the kitchen, dripping everywhere. Sure enough, Hula was on her hind legs, happily counter surfing, her head deep in the pot the stew had cooked in.

Okay, okay, I know we should have put the thing away, but still, she needs to have some manners. The other dogs don't do that. "Hula!" I yelled. "Get out of there! You are such a dirty rotten terrible girl!" I chased her out of the kitchen and down the hall just to let her know I meant business. I stomped back to the kitchen, got the Scat Mat out and slapped it on the floor at the entrance to the kitchen. The Scat Mat is a clear plastic mat with a mild electric charge to discourage animals from getting on counters or other places they are not supposed to be. I usually put it on the lowest setting but this time I meant business and cranked it up to high. That would fix her.

I headed back to the bath, muttering under my breath, climbed back in the tub and tried to relax. Within five minutes my cell phone rang with another emergency call. By then I was beyond caring. I grabbed my towel and headed for the bedroom to put on my uniform again. As I passed the darkened kitchen I realized the window was open so I walked in to shut it. HOLY MOTHER OF GOD, WHAT WAS THAT! I leapt into the air, limbs flailing, heart pounding. It took a moment to realize what had happened. The shock was mild, but in my exhausted state, my bare wet feet on the Scat Mat was an experience I would rather not repeat. It did, however, effectively cure me from leaving food out.

8. Big Bad Gus

I continued working with Annie, the mustang, almost every day after work. She was coming along so nicely. She could be calmly tied now and once I could groom her all over her body I started working with her feet. I would pass a long cotton rope around her leg up high and then hold each end and stand back to a safe distance. Holding each end I'd work the rope gently up and down her leg to accustom her to the feeling. Then I would lower it to below her fetlock and apply steady pressure. When she lifted the foot I released it, gradually increasing the time I held each foot up. Eventually, I was able to clean and handle her feet with ease. I was especially tickled about it because Bob, my supervisor at work, had teased me about getting an ungentled mustang. "That's all good," he said, with a grin. "But let's see you pick up her feet." Annie was doing so well I had Nikki come out and snap of photo of me holding one of her rear feet up to show Bob. I was proud of our progress.

One evening, Nikki helped me put Annie away and feed the horses and we were headed in to dinner when I got a call on standby. Sheriff's dispatch informed me of a woman who had reported being attacked by a pit bull on

Florida Drive. I took her information and dialed the number. I don't get too excited by "attack" calls until I get the whole scoop because people use the word so freely. I think of an attack as a full-on mauling as opposed to a bite, but it's often used to mean a dog barked at them from fifty feet away. And sure enough, my caller described getting out of her car at her house, seeing the dog running toward her and rushing inside. "Were you hurt?" I asked.

"No."

"Can you see the dog now?"

"No.

"Do you need to go out again tonight?"

"No."

"Well, thank you so much for calling and call us back in the morning if the dog is still around."

Gratefully, I settled back down to my dinner, happy to spend some time with Paul and the kids. Five minutes later dispatch called again and reported that a man and his son were both attacked by a pit bull on Florida Drive. The dispatcher sounded slightly alarmed and said they were sending a deputy and wanted me to respond. I told them I was on my way and hurried out to the truck hoping I hadn't blown it by not responding to the first call. Our protocol is that we don't respond after hours to strays unless they are injured or aggressive but this was sounding serious.

Florida Drive is a largely Hispanic neighborhood about five miles from my house. I was halfway there when the dispatcher brought me up on the radio. This time she sounded frantic, which was highly unusual. These people deal with all manner of catastrophe with unflappable serenity. Accidents, robberies, rapes, stabbings and murder are dispatched with complete calm. This time the woman on the radio almost yelled through the receiver. "I've got multiple people attacked by the dog, officers on scene and I need you there immediately. They may need to shoot it."

"I'm about five minutes out," I replied. "I'll be there as soon as possible." I stomped on the gas and the truck shot toward the deepening sunset.

A few minutes later I pulled onto Florida Drive. Sheriff's deputies with flashing lights had the road closed but urgently flagged me through. I pulled into a driveway surrounded by patrol cars. The sun was just about down and my headlights illuminated a highly charged scene. Two deputies had rifles sighted and aimed in front of them. Their bodies were leaned forward, the picture of tension, with the barrels of the guns only about two feet from a huge dog that lay immobilized on the concrete.

The dog was dark gray and one of the largest dogs I had ever seen. He wasn't a pit bull but some sort of Mastiff. His captors had somehow managed to get a long shovel handle through the dog's collar and, with two guys on each end, had twisted his collar until they had forced him to the ground and subdued him. They had also trussed up his rear legs with a piece of thick yellow rope. As I approached with my catch pole in hand, I saw the dog's tail twitch a couple of times. That sometimes happens when an animal is choked, but it still made me wonder. I slipped the noose over the huge head and told the men to remove the shovel handle. I asked them to untie his legs but they were too nervous to do it. I couldn't do it while holding the pole, so we decided to carry the heavy dog the few feet to my truck and managed to heave him onto the blanket in the back. I was surprised to note that he was neutered. Not too many dogs on this side of town were.

Once the dog was safely confined I was able to survey the rest of the scene. Besides the deputies at least ten men stood around. I scanned them for bite wounds, blood and injuries. I was expecting total carnage and hadn't found it yet.

A middle-aged man stepped forward. He said his name was Manuel and that he was the one who had called. I asked him what had happened. "My son, Isidro, and I were working in the yard." He indicated another man, not the child that I had expected. "And the dog come running and attack my son and me."

"How did he attack you?" I asked.

"He jump at my son's neck and face and then mine." Manuel

53

pantomimed a dog leaping up, jaws wide and going for the throat. "We scream and our neighbors come to help and the dog attack them, too."

"Were any of you bitten?" I asked. The men all shook their heads.

"How did you keep from getting bitten?"

"We fight heem off," Manuel answered.

"What did you fight him off with?"

"Our hands," said Manuel.

"Are you sure the dog was being aggressive and not trying to play?"

"Oh no," said Manuel, with sincerity. "He try to keel us."

With a feeling of disbelief I thanked the deputies and said goodnight. It was pitch black as I drove away pondering the situation. Was the dog really a killer? The chances of these guys fighting off this monster dog with their bare hands without being injured were pretty slim, but I knew that anything could happen. I decided to leave the dog on the blanket in my truck overnight rather than risk trying to kennel him by myself late at night at the shelter where no one could help me if I got into trouble. He probably weighed as much as I did.

As I pulled into my driveway, I remembered that the dog's rear legs were tied. I certainly couldn't leave him overnight like that. Paul was home, so at least he could call 911 if the dog went berserk on me.

As I stepped out of my truck I heard a loud THUMP THUMP THUMP coming from the back. Paul and our son Scott came out to see me as I grabbed the flashlight and opened the exterior door. The dog box is made with double doors for safety and once the main door was open we could see a huge pink tongue lapping at the wire grid between us while the rhythmic banging of his tail on the metal sides continued.

I sighed with annoyance. My killer dog appeared to be an overgrown pussycat. I greeted him affectionately and attempted to shove his fat head out of the way so I could cut his legs free. He licked me ecstatically and shook my whole truck with his display of delight as I freed his limbs. I was relieved to see he didn't seem injured by his run-in with the shovel handle and rope. I surveyed his thick, muscular neck in awe. It was a wonder they had succeeded in slowing him down at all. I gave him some food and water and he settled on his blanket in the truck for the night, apparently tired by the evening's excitement.

At the shelter the next morning, I slipped a lead on the dog and jumped him out of the truck. He was thrilled to be free and lunged around like a circus elephant, almost yanking me off my feet. Anne, one of the especially dog-savvy shelter techs, approached with amusement at the sight of this giant goofball. The dog leapt at her face with his jaw gaping wide and all his pearly whites glistening as he tried to lick her. Huge paws raked her chest as I attempted to rein him in. Anne tried to shove him off but was laughing too hard. The dog was just wildly affectionate, exuberant and untrained, not to mention as big as a donkey.

I could easily picture the scene of the previous night from the view of the dog's "victims." Here they were quietly trying to finish some yard work before it was dark and this monster shoots out of the gloom and leaps for their throats with a mouthful of big teeth. He rushes from one to another in total delight as they pummel him harmlessly with their fists and run around in a panic searching for a weapon, sure their lives are over. It was easy to see how someone could be terrified of a dog that size with his dark coloring and big fangs, especially at night. But the men didn't seem traumatized, more like thrilled to be alive, proud and empowered to have fought off a vicious animal with their bare hands. I had detected a note of triumph in them as I was leaving the scene; they seemed to truly believe they had narrowly escaped death and had a great story to tell their families.

Later that day a young man named Juan came to claim the dog. He lived a few blocks from the scene of the chaos and had no idea of the near disaster his dog had been involved in or how close the dog had come to being shot. I was trying to explain to Juan how important it was not to let his dog loose. He was a nice guy but was having trouble understanding me with his limited English.

"You have to keep your dog in your yard. He was almost shot by the cops last night, and people thought he was trying to attack them." I partly yelled and partly used hand signals to get the point across.

Juan looked surprised. He stroked his dog's broad head, and the dog panted up at him with his big dopey face. Then Juan looked at me. "They think Gus try to bite them?" He was stumped by this news.

"Yes, they almost shot Gus last night."

As I spoke Gus flopped over on his back and started rolling around the lobby floor kicking his legs in the air like a complete dufus. Juan looked at me doubtfully, shrugged his shoulders and called to his pet. Gus leapt to his feet and catapulted toward the exit. Juan's head snapped back as he was yanked through the door and was gone.

9. The Bengal Cat

"Shirley, have you seen the cat I picked up?" my coworker, Leslie, asked one morning at work. "It's a beautiful Bengal in really bad shape."

I was researching my calls for the day ahead and asked what had happened to him. The cat had been hit by a car on a busy road, she explained. Someone had seen him lying on the pavement and called the shelter. When Leslie arrived he lay flat-out on the roadside. He wasn't moving, but when she started to scoop him up she was shocked to see him take a slow, gasping breath. She bundled him up and rushed him to the nearest emergency vet clinic. The cat had severe head trauma, a badly broken jaw, a fractured pelvis and other injuries and stayed at the clinic overnight before being transferred to our shelter clinic.

I've always liked Bengals. A hybrid of a domestic cat and an Asian wild cat, they have beautiful markings. I hurried into the back to our clinic to see him and found him sleeping on a blanket in the treatment room, his head swollen and misshapen, his jaw shaved from surgery. Due to his injuries, he was unable to eat, sit up or walk. He was so seriously injured, in fact, the staff had

57

questioned attempting to save him. His brain injury alone was enough to kill him. Even if he survived he might never be functional again.

But he was so obviously someone's pet. Clean, shiny fur, young, neutered. He was also de-clawed, something I'm not a fan of, but it showed that someone went to considerable expense for him and was probably looking for him.

When the cat was finally well enough to be released from the vet clinic he still needed extensive rehab, so I took him home to foster. He had to be kept on cage rest and fed gruel for weeks while his body healed. Nikki named him James.

James's daily nursing care was time-consuming. Nikki and Shay helped me carefully syringe a liquid diet down his poor busted-up mouth several times a day. He also needed twice daily pain medication and antibiotics, but he was an affectionate, adorable cat and we were soon smitten with his engaging ways.

I just kept thinking that someone must be missing him. His photograph and description were posted on the shelter website with all the other strays, and I combed the lost and found ads of the local newspapers and Craigslist.org. I also patrolled the area where he was found for lost cat posters but found nothing.

A month later, James was much improved but still kept indoors at home because of his head injury. He was healing well but was still a little "dopey" and needed ongoing care. One day, I was patrolling in the neighborhood where he was picked up and decided to check out some condominiums located just behind the road where James had been hit. On a whim, I began knocking on doors. The second person I talked to had lost a Bengal cat a month before. He was a young man, probably in his late twenties. He described James to a tee and even showed me a photo. He said he had paid $600 for the Bengal as a kitten.

I had found James's owner! I was so excited I could hardly believe it. I began to question him. Why hadn't he come looking at the shelter? He said he was certain the cat had been stolen so he hadn't searched. I explained about

James's injuries and his ongoing care.

In my enthusiasm at finding James's owner I didn't realize right that away that I was the only one who was excited. If it was my pet found after being lost for months, I probably would have been crying, frantic, begging to see him immediately. But everyone reacts differently. I gave the guy directions to the shelter and arranged to meet him at the shelter with James. Oh no, he said, he wouldn't be able to pick up the cat until the next day because he was busy, and how much was it going to cost him? He added that he had a rambunctious three-year-old son and would that be a problem with the cat's injuries?

As I drove to the shelter I began to consider the situation. I had a bad feeling about the whole thing. At the shelter I added up all of James's vet bills, impound fees and board. It came to many hundreds of dollars. We would have tried to work with him or take payments if he had been desperate to get his pet back or had shown some real interest, but as expected, when I called him with the total he decided not to claim James and signed the cat over to the shelter.

That night as I stroked James's shiny spotted coat and listened to his blissful purring, I wondered why people pay huge amounts of money for a pet and develop no attachment to them. I think it's often a status thing and they forget that a great deal of care and expense goes into having an animal. It should be a lifelong commitment.

James bumped my chin with his forehead, breaking my reverie. He gazed into my face with his emerald green eyes and purred louder. His head was still a bit misshapen, he was missing a couple of teeth and he wasn't the sharpest tool in the shed but he was absolutely lovable. We held a family meeting and decided that after all he had been through we couldn't part with him.

James continued to improve, but it was clear he was always going to have some deficits due to his head injury. He loved every living thing and purred happily while throwing himself at everyone he met, but he was klutzy and prone to falling off things. We live in a safe area set well back from busy roads, so our other cats are allowed out during the day, but James had no claws and couldn't find his way in from the front porch, so he wasn't allowed outside.

Sadly, though, that doesn't mean he didn't go outside. He loved to explore and would attempt to bolt out the door every chance he got. A few times, he did slip out and disappear, turning up days or even weeks later some miles away. Because of his tag and good luck someone always called us to come and get him. He would be thrilled to see us, acting more like a dog than a cat with the effusiveness of his greeting. I don't think he intended to run away, he just didn't have the sense to find his way home because of his head injury.

One day, I was working with Annie when James apparently snuck out of the house. I had been trying to accustom Annie to the saddle, and she was extremely hesitant. It's funny how some things she accepted in only a few tries but others seemed to take forever. I had her tied and was taking a lot of time to let her see the saddle near her. I kept it in sight while I groomed her. I had the straps and stirrups tied up so there was nothing to flop around and scare her. Finally, I'd managed to lay the saddle across her back, talking quietly to her and praising her. I was just about to remove it when she exploded straight into the air, knocking me out of the way. The saddle went flying. Annie leapt around in a panic, fighting the railroad tie with all she had.

It took me a moment to realize what had happened. There was James, almost right underneath the horse. He had no doubt eagerly tried to rub against her legs, and she had been terrified by his sudden appearance. I grabbed Annie's halter with one hand and tried to calm her while using the toe of my boot to boost James to safety without getting kicked myself. Breathless, I quickly scooped James into my arms and cradled him. My heart pounded while he purred contentedly in my arms. The near catastrophe (cat-astrophe?) had me shaken and weak and he was completely clueless! He could have so easily been killed. Whatever sense of self-preservation he had seemed to have been knocked right out of him by his run-in with the car.

That evening we all sat down and discussed checking for James before opening the door. "It's annoying, Mom," Scott said, rolling his eyes. "He hides and then he bolts out the minute you open the door."

"I know, but we all just have to be more careful," I said.

60

Nikki scooped James up in her arms and headed for her room.

10. Jerk Bitch Angel Hero

The horses trotted up the road in front of me as I followed with flashers on. Cars were stacked up behind me, people honking impatiently. Some tried to pass. One guy yelled, "Out of the way, jerk!" He zoomed around me and then had to throw his brakes on as he almost collided with the horses. What did he think? I just drive around town at five miles an hour with my flashers on for entertainment? I like hearing people honk and call me names for kicks? Jeez people, get a grip.

We were approaching a blind corner on a busy highway and I fretted about what to do. There were five horses loose and I wasn't sure where they lived. I suspected they came from a property up ahead and to the left. I decided to take the risk and try to get ahead of them and turn them into the driveway.

I waited for a break in traffic, shot around the horses and got ahead of them. I jumped out of the truck waving my arms, and fortunately they turned down the driveway and away from traffic. I followed them toward an expensive looking home and when they ran around back and jumped over a break in the fence I breathed a sigh of relief.

A pale scruffy-haired young man came out of the house wearing nothing but baggy sweat pants. He squinted and blinked in the bright sun until he saw me. "What the hell are you doing here?"

"Are those your horses?" I asked, pointing at the herd.

"What about it?"

"They were out on the highway dodging cars. It looks like you need to repair your fence."

"The horses pushed it down. I can't do anything about that," he said with a sneer.

Who raised this kid? I thought. He needs to learn some manners. "It's the owner's responsibility to confine their animals," I said. "I'll need to see some I.D. and ask you to sign a written warning notice and repair your fence."

"Lady, you obviously don't know anything about horses." His voice was filled with sarcasm. "They weigh a thousand pounds. They do whatever they want. I'm not signing any notice."

At that moment an SUV roared into the drive and shuddered to a stop. Out jumped a woman who was an older and, if possible, even snottier version of junior. She shook her frosted hair away from her heavily made-up eyes and started in on me. "What the hell is going on here? Why are you harassing my son? What is going on?" A little Jack Russell Terrier in the vehicle barked and wagged his tail at me as she yelled.

"Ma'am, your horses were out on the highway. They nearly caused an accident."

The woman cut me off before I could finish and began to berate me at length. I made several gallant attempts to speak while she cussed and carried on and called me an idiot. She made sure to mention that her family owned a prominent business in town, as if that was going to make a difference. I finally had to threaten to call the sheriff's office since I also needed to cite her for her dog's expired license. The little dog was the only friendly face on the place.

"Go ahead and call the cops, you bitch!" she snapped.

63

But when I started to dial my cell phone, she snarled, "Oh fine, just give me the damn thing and let's get this over with." She signed the citation and a warning notice for the horses and stomped off toward the house, catching her high heeled-shoe on a hose and stumbling as she went, which brought further swearing.

It was a relief to drive away. I had Luci with me in the truck and she laid her head across the center console. I stroked her sleek black coat, feeling my breathing grow steady again as I headed to my next call. This one was supposed to be a kitten rescue. Rescuing a kitten sounded just my speed after dealing with Ms. Dragon-lady-horse-owner-from-hell.

When I arrived at the kitten call, the kindly older woman explained that she had been feeding a stray cat and intended to spay her but the cat had given birth high in the attic of the barn before she could make an appointment for the surgery. The woman planned to keep the mother and find homes for the kittens. She wanted to bring them in the house where they would be safe and accustomed to people. The mother cat was very tame and friendly, but the newborn kittens were out of reach and the weather was heating up, making it extremely hot in the attic.

I climbed into the crawlspace above the barn. There was the mother cat snuggled with her kittens far back in the eves and out of reach. She purred proudly and licked her babies as I inched closer on my belly. I was still about a foot short and the space was too narrow for a net. The newborns were too small to get with my catch pole. Even my cat grabbers, an animal-handling tool with a long padded grip, were too large. I wracked my brain for a way to extend my reach.

Meanwhile, the caller waited hopefully as I brainstormed. A possibility came to me. "Do you have a long pair of kitchen tongs?"

"Oh, I do!" she cried. "I'll be right back."

The heat was becoming oppressive as I lay there under the tin roof. I knew that if this didn't work the kittens would be in trouble.

Moments later, I was handed a long set of tongs. I reached in and, smooth as silk, scooped up each of the four kittens and placed them in a small carrier I had brought with me. They were so cute I had to cuddle the last one to my cheek and admire its tiny pink nose and fuzzy face before placing it next to its siblings. Mama immediately climbed in after them and when I passed them to the waiting caller, she was delighted. "Oh you are such an angel, how can I ever thank you!" She gave me a warm hug and insisted I come in and have a slice of homemade apple pie with ice cream while she got the kitties set up in a cozy bathroom.

I was feeling pretty good as I drove away, that is, until I noticed a motion inside a vehicle coming toward me on the road. As it grew closer I could see the old white-haired driver urgently flipping me the bird as if his life depended on it. His face was scrunched in a grimace and he was putting everything he had into the gesture as he glared at me through the windshield and pumped his middle finger. Then he passed by and was gone. I didn't think I recognized him, but who knows? I may have cited him or something at some point. Or did he just hate animal control as a whole? I puzzled over it for a few moments, momentarily deflated. It seems that people either love us or hate us, there isn't much in between. As a rule, the responsible animal lovers love us and the jerks hate us. I can live with that.

That night, Scott and I were cleaning up after dinner and chatting about school when I received a call from the police department. I was on call and dispatch informed me that a disabled woman needed help with her pet parakeet; it was tangled in some sort of toy. That sounded a little strange, and I gave her a call to try to get more information. The poor woman sounded utterly distraught. I couldn't quite understand the problem but I told her I was on my way. I hated to leave the kids, but they're supportive of my job. "You have to help the poor lady with her parakeet, Mom," Nikki said, and Scott and Shay gave me an encouraging hug as I headed out.

The woman lived on the fourth floor of an older apartment building. I rode the elevator up and headed down the musty, dimly lit hallway to number 414. I knocked and heard a woman's voice. "Come in!" I opened the door. The

65

woman sat in a wheelchair dressed in a faded pink nightgown, tears streaming down her cheeks. She pointed anxiously at the floor of the tiny apartment. Little Petie was fighting some sort of battle on the well-worn carpet. His neck was through one of the links of a colorful plastic chain that attached the toy to the cage and was struggling desperately. "I was able to get it off the cage but it's caught around his neck," she said, her voice shaking.

I grabbed a dishtowel and picked up the tiny creature in it, avoiding the sharp, curved beak. Parakeets can bite like the dickens when they are scared and I had no doubt this little guy was upset. Birds are also exceedingly fragile; one wrong move and they're injured or dead. Holding the head gently between my finger and thumb I felt through the feathers for the surprisingly skinny neck encased in the link. It was hard to imagine how he had gotten into this predicament but it only took a moment to work the link free and release Petie. He flew immediately to the woman's shoulder, startling her, at which point she burst into tears. "Oh, how can I ever thank you! You are my hero." She turned her weathered face to the bird and he nibbled companionably on her wet cheek. "He's my dearest, dearest friend," she said. "I just don't know what I would do without him."

That night, in bed, Paul and I chatted about my day. "Well," he said, "there aren't many jobs where you get flipped off, hugged, and called a jerk, a bitch, an angel, and a hero all in the same day." He had a point, but that's public service for you. He wrapped me in his arms and drifted off to sleep, while I lay awake for a while, thinking. My family is such a source of support and comfort for me. Having Paul to talk to helps me process the day and cope with the stress. I finally slept, too, safe in Paul's embrace.

11. Nikki Saves a Life

I hurried into the house on my lunch break to check on my latest pregnant foster dog. I usually have an extra dog or two in my care and moms with litters of pups are my specialty. This one was more of a worry than most, though. The Pekingese lay in her bed in the living room looking like a bloated sausage. Sushi had come to the shelter with several other dogs when her owner was hospitalized and unable to care for them. The shelter's not the best place for a dog in her condition, so I brought her home. Pekingese have fat heads and narrow hips and often need cesareans to deliver. There's usually someone home but today everyone else was out.

I took care of all the dogs and headed back out for the second half of my workday. At least I was working in the area and could check in frequently. Nikki called at 2:30 to say that she was home and I reminded her to be on "Sushi Watch." I felt much better with her there and was able to concentrate on work.

At around 3:30 my cell rang. "Mom, I think Sushi's getting close, she's really panting and fussing around."

Great. I had just gotten tied up with some loose cattle quite a ways

67

away and couldn't leave. "Please keep a close watch on her and call me if anything happens," I told her. It would probably be a while. Sometimes pregnant moms fuss around like that for hours or even days. I turned my attention back to the cows. They had wandered out on the roadway and were grazing contentedly in the ditch. I got out of the truck and shooed them away from the busy main road, walking behind them and looking for a place to confine them while I searched for the owner. Five minutes later, Nikki called again. "She had a puppy!"

"That's good news," I said. "Can you see if it's breathing?"

"Yeah, it's squeaking and moving around and Sushi's licking it." Nikki has seen foster puppies born before and supervised another birth with me gone in the past. Usually if they can pass the first puppy it's a good sign. I was so relieved that she was off to a good start and hoped to avoid a caesarean.

"Thanks for being there, sweetie. Just watch and make sure she's taking care of it." I hung up as one of the cows tried to dodge around me. I ran to cut her off. The sun beat down and I could feel the sweat trickling inside my shirt as a woman pulled up in a car. I flagged her down and asked her if she knew where the cows lived. She pointed to a field farther up the road. At least we were headed in the right direction. I pushed some loose strands of hair out of my face and continued to head them toward home.

Nikki called again fifteen minutes later to tell me another pup had been born and things were going fine. What a relief. The cows turned down a long driveway ahead of me and I followed them toward an old farmhouse. Banging on the weathered front door brought a barrel-chested old guy in suspenders and jeans to the entry. The cows belonged to him and we were able to get them back into the pasture without much trouble.

My phone rang again as I was leaving. This time Nikki's voice sounded urgent. "Mom, she just had another puppy but it's not moving."

"Can you see if it's breathing?" I asked, gunning it for home.

"I don't think so. What should I do?"

"Grab it in one of the towels next to Sushi's pen, make sure the sack is

68

off its face, then suction out its mouth with the bulb syringe," I instructed. I whipped past a speed limit sign and glanced at my odometer. Oops. Better slow down. Nikki's voice came back on the line.

"Okay, I did, but it's still not doing anything."

"Suction it again," I told her, "and then hold the head down and rub it really vigorously with the towel." I heard her fumble with the phone and then pick it up again. "It's not doing anything, Mom. It's still totally limp and kind of blue."

"Keep trying, honey. You have to be kind of rough to stimulate breathing. I'm on my way."

I pulled into the driveway a few minutes later and ran for the house. Nikki came to the door carrying a tiny puppy still wrapped in a towel. With a big smile she held it up for me to see. It was nice and pink and moving and starting to squeal. I hugged her and then checked on Sushi and the other newborns. They looked great so I headed back to work, leaving Nikki in charge. Sushi gave birth to three more puppies that day.

That evening when I got home Sushi was relaxed and happily nursing her babies while Shay kept an eye on her from the couch. Mickey was making dinner, Paul and Scott weren't home yet, and Nikki was in her room doing homework. Shay and I visited for a few minutes, I gave Sushi a cuddle under her chin, told her she was a good girl and headed out to work with Annie for a while before dinner.

Annie walked up to greet me in the pasture. I find it fascinating that she's so sociable now. After many months of work I can walk right up to her and put a halter on. Since she no longer has to wear a halter all the time I turned her out with the geldings, where they fell over themselves to gain her favor. She mostly ignored them, but I think she enjoyed having more room to move around and being part of a herd again. I was surprised she shows no concern when I take her away from them to work with her. Roanie is practically hysterical every time I take him away from the group and he spazzes around, whinnying frantically for a few minutes. Annie had no such worries. She doesn't seembonded with the other horses. I'm sad about that and wonder if it comes from being separated from her herd in the wild. Mares often stay with the same family group their whole lives.

I brought Annie up to the railroad tie, clipped her to it and began to groom her from head to toe. She stood quietly as I worked. Her coat was starting to shine, the thick mane and tail rippled, and it was relaxing for us both as I brushed and combed her and picked her feet. I led her to the round pen, unclipped her and walked to the center. I clicked my tongue softly to her and she began to walk her circle around me. After a few minutes I clicked to her again and said "trot." She picked up the pace and I stood mesmerized by her graceful movement and flowing tail. Ten minutes later I coaxed her up to a canter for a bit and then asked her to "whoa." She stopped on a dime and stood waiting while I came to her and praised her. I asked her to reverse and started all again. As she worked, I felt the tensions of the day ease. There was something hypnotic about watching her trot around me while the sun set over the barn and the swallows swooped in and out in the fading light.

12. Some Days Are Like That

I kind of hate it when an emergency call comes first thing in the morning. The job can be so demanding that the early morning time to go over our calls, work on reports, drink some coffee and prepare for the day can be so helpful. Also, the early calls are often for deer that have been hit by cars in the morning commute and are suffering and need to be euthanized. Not my favorite way to start the day.

Sure enough, I had been at work just long enough to down a couple of cups of coffee but not long enough to wake up when a deer call came in. I called Luci from her bed under my desk and headed for the truck. It was nearly forty-five minutes away, and by the time I reached the area where the deer was supposed to be I was urgently reminded of all the coffee I had consumed. I drove up and down the remote, heavily wooded road for another twenty minutes without finding the unfortunate animal and by then I was desperate for relief.

There was no public restroom anywhere around and I had reached the point of agony. I parked on the side of the road and hurried down a nearby deer trail, threw off my duty belt and dropped my pants. Seconds later, a car door

71

slammed on the road above me. I struggled to yank up my uniform pants but they got tangled in my heavy-duty belt and long radio cord. Damn! I could hear a male voice calling hello as he came down the trail. A panicked moment of frantic scrambling resulted in one very disheveled animal control officer with an un-tucked shirt, radio cord wrapped around my leg, and hair partly pulled free from my ponytail by a wayward branch. A tall, young firefighter came around the corner on the trail and stopped short when he saw me. There was a moment of awkward silence as we stared at each other and then we both burst out laughing. "I saw your truck. Are you looking for the deer?" he asked, red-faced.

"Well, I thought it might have come down here," I answered, lamely. He laughed again. "Follow me, I'll show you where it is." He headed back up the path as I tried to put myself back together.

By the time we reached the road I was somewhat acceptable again. He pointed out where the deer had crawled back in the bushes. I never would have seen her without his assistance. She had already died before I arrived, which was better than her suffering while I searched for her and bared my butt to the world.

It had been far worse a few weeks earlier when a big beautiful buck was hit on the freeway during rush hour. He was flopping around in traffic and California Highway Patrol had cars stopped in both directions. I had to drive quite a ways on the shoulder to get around all the stopped cars and when I finally pulled up, I'm sure that all the eight million drivers stuck there watching the poor animal thought I was there to save it. I so wish I could have pulled up and strapped the buck to a stretcher and rushed with lights flashing to the nearest deer hospital. Instead, the audience was treated to the sight of Blondie getting out of her truck with a rifle and cracking the poor thing before dragging it off the freeway and driving away.

I put the deer out of my mind as I concentrated on my next call. The man whose home I was headed for had a reputation as hot tempered and impossible to deal with. Mr. Sigura lived in an elite country neighborhood and allowed his Doberman to run loose and bother his neighbors. Other officers had left notices on his door and received hostile messages from him on their

72

voicemail. Meanwhile, the dog, Thor, had continued to go onto several neighbor's properties, defecating, digging up landscaping and chasing cats. Worst of all, Thor had started to feel that he owned the neighborhood and began to defend it from the rightful owners by barking and growling at them on their own property. Dobermans can be delightful animals, but they were bred to be protective and can be a menace in the wrong hands.

Enough neighbors had sent in written complaint statements to pursue an abatement order. I read through the statements and then contacted each of them for further information. Each person described the dog owner as a completely hostile man who did whatever he wanted and screamed at anyone who got in his way. He had apparently run off the fire marshal after burning leaves without a permit, threatened several of his neighbors and then screamed in the face of a deputy who responded when they called the cops on him. A real jewel of a man. I wasn't really looking forward to showing up and telling this guy this was his last chance to comply with the leash law before his neighbors take him to court.

I pride myself on putting people at ease, helping them feel comfortable and helping the hotheads of the world calm down. Most of the time I have good luck with people like that. Often people start yelling and swearing when I show up and by the time I leave they're thanking me for my help and promising to keep Kilo or Bubba confined. I started planning my strategy so I would have Mr. Sigura eating out of my hand when I was done with him. I would smile, offer some helpful suggestions and tell him I was sure he could manage the problem without it going to court. I might even offer a comforting pat on the shoulder as I explained that I had a Doberman, too. Luci was riding in the truck with me and he would probably want to see her. Heck, he would probably even call my supervisor and tell him what a terrific gal I was.

So I was feeling fairly confident as I pulled up to the huge mansion surrounded by gorgeous landscaping. One of the neighbors had told me that if he was home his red Ferrari would be in the driveway. I have to admit I was slightly relieved the car wasn't there. Children's toys and shoes littered the large

73

stone porch as I approached the palatial front door. I hoped he controlled his temper with his kids. Maybe I would get lucky and talk to a Mrs. Sigura, assuming there was one.

No answer came to my knock at the door, and I could see Thor barking in his kennel across the yard as I posted a notice on the door. At least he wasn't loose now. Maybe Mr. Sigura was already planning to comply.

It was starting to mist lightly and from where I was standing it appeared that Thor had no shelter in his kennel. I decided to drive farther up the private road in an attempt to see the kennel better. I pulled out of the drive and went farther up the road where there was a clear view of the yard. As I suspected, there was no shelter and Thor had no way to get out of the elements. Apparently, he slept inside at night and was only in the kennel when no one was home, but he still needed shelter during the day. I turned the truck around and started to head back down the road.

Right about then a red Ferrari whipped into the driveway. A smallish man with blazing red hair leapt out of the vehicle and glanced at me as I pulled in behind him. To my surprise he didn't acknowledge my presence or come toward me, but stalked rapidly away from me across the yard. I got out of the truck and called to him. "Sir, can I talk to you for a minute?" He didn't respond. I realized then he was headed for Thor's kennel. Reaching it, he threw the gate wide and said something to the dog that I couldn't make out. Thor burst loose from his confines and raced toward me. It appeared that Mr. Sigura had just sicked his dog on me! Thor's body language was highly aroused, alert and more curious than aggressive, so I cautiously stood my ground as he raced up and began giving me a rapid inspection, sniffing my clothes intently.

I turned my attention back to Mr. Sigura and my alarm grew. He was coming at me almost as fast as the dog had, but his body language was that of someone about to kick some serious butt. He looked furious, his face as red as his hair, and both nearly as red as his car. He began to scream at me as Thor circled. "Get off my property! Go on get out of here!" The face contorted into a mask of rage as he grew closer until he was yelling up into my face. "Get off my property right now! I will have you arrested. I will make a citizen's arrest, get off my property!"

The man was probably only about 5'4" tall, but his hostility was huge and frightening. His pale blue eyes bugged inches from mine as he stood on tiptoe, screaming at me to get off his property before he called the police and threatening to make a citizen's arrest. I hadn't even told him why I was there! Was he going to attempt to take me down? He was definitely in my personal space. If he grabbed me I was prepared to crack him over the cranium with my asp, though I worried Thor would pick up on his agitation and get aggressive. But the big dog seemed to take it all in stride.

I stood up straighter, clutched my paperwork and fingered my can of pepper spray while trying to get a word in edgewise. I kind of wanted to pepper him just to shut him up for a minute, but it wasn't worth losing my job over this no matter how he continued to shout aggressively over everything I said.

My heart was pounding out of my chest and I realized I could be putting my safety in jeopardy. I quickly wrote "refused to sign" on the documents and tore off his copy to hand to him. He waved it away and continued his tirade. I said, "You have been served," and dropped the paper on the ground. At that, he turned on his heel and walked rapidly away, still screaming, Thor trotting at his heels.

Dobermans are usually very sensitive, but fortunately Thor seemed unperturbed by his violent owner. I, on the other hand, didn't draw a breath until I reached the main road. I pulled over on a wide turnout and stroked Luci's silky coat for a few minutes, until I stopped shaking. The truck had been parked some distance from the confrontation, so Luci hadn't seen what was going on. She could see I was upset, though, and she cuddled close.

I had rarely witnessed such irrational behavior, let alone from someone like him. Maybe from a crack-head or someone really drunk or drugged out when I took their dog away or something. This man didn't seem to be under the influence of anything but anger. So much for my "We're going to be pals and aren't I great with people" fantasy.

What really chapped my hide is that less than two weeks later, my coworker, Rich Owens, had a call there. Mr. Sigura behaved like a perfect gentleman, with a whole lot of "Yes, sir" and "No, sir" and "Of course I'll keep the dog on my property" and "Where would you like me to sign, sir." Rich even cited him for licensing! This guy kissed his ass. I was so annoyed. Did I mention that Rich is about 6'4" tall and built like a linebacker? He could have crushed Mr. Sigura under his heel! I have never wanted to be anyone else, but there have been a few times I could see the advantage of being built like Rich. Who knows, maybe Mr. Sigura just has personal issues with women, neighbors and cops but not with burly male animal control officers.

As much as it might help to be built like Rich, on some calls it's an advantage to be a woman. Women tend to be less intimidating, which can be helpful with a scared dog. On countless calls where one of our male officers has called for backup to capture a loose dog, a woman officer has been able to coax the dog in within minutes. On one memorable occasion, Nikki was riding along with me when fellow officer Jim Nielson called for assistance with a dog he'd been trying to catch for forty-five minutes. He had coaxed, sweet-talked and offered treats without success. Nikki joked that we would probably catch the dog in five minutes. As I arrived on the scene I could see a little red-nosed pit bull running hard toward me with Jim following at a distance in his truck. I opened my door and called and made kissy noises at her. She rocketed straight toward me and scrambled up into my lap while looking over her shoulder for Jim. "Help, save me from that bad man!" was her obvious plea. As I slipped a lead over her head, I heard Jim's voice on the radio. "That's just not right."

13. The Great Baby Duck Rescue

It happens every spring. A mother duck sits patiently on her well-hidden nest and then hatches out a dozen tiny and adorable ducklings. They follow her obediently in a perfectly ordered line until she walks across the nearest drainage grate where half of them plop through the spaces to the depths below.

This time it happened in a senior mobile home park and it was news of epic proportions. Most of the residents were retired and had a lot of time on their hands. They got great pleasure from watching their feathered friends, and this was a true catastrophe.

A group of white-haired ladies gathered around the offending grate clasping their hands and fussing anxiously as I pulled up. Several spoke at once, as I assessed the situation. One offered me a little net she had made using a coat hanger, safety pins and her pink nylon underwear. The woman wasn't very big but the pink undies were what Paul's mom would call "large Marge" underwear and if they'd been attached to a longer handle they might have been helpful. I admired her ingenuity and showed her the long-handled net I always carry in my truck.

I have some pretty good duck-rescuing tricks up my sleeve, but the grate was too heavy to lift by hand. I called maintenance and a nice-looking 60ish gentleman arrived shortly with a tractor. The ladies practically swooned as he saved the day by removing the grate. He basked in their attention while I peered into the space six feet below.

The babies huddled together in a shaft of sunlight, peeping frantically for their mama and scrambling over each other as I maneuvered my net. If I wasn't careful they would run down the long narrow pipes and be lost. Happily, this bunch stayed together and I managed to scoop them up in a group.

Now it was time to find mama. The mother duck had been quacking desperately from the sidelines but she had finally given up and fled with the rest of her family when the tractor arrived. Several of my worried onlookers offered suggestions and followed me as we looked for mama, the babies still held aloft in the net. The concern on the weathered faces was evident as we searched. What good was a rescue if the family couldn't be reunited?

My sweet little white-haired friend, still clutching her panty net, stayed right by my side as we wandered hopefully around the park, peering behind garden gnomes and gardenia bushes. The babies peeped continuously and I hoped that mama would hear them, but I was beginning to worry.

I had just about given up when a small brown duck with several babies in tow appeared and began calling frantically as she ran toward us across a nearby expanse of lawn. The ducklings in the net peeped eagerly in response and I quickly tipped them out on the grass. It was beautiful to see mother and babies run toward each other, calling continuously. The youngsters looked so comical, their little necks stretched out as they ran with tiny wings held aloft.

Reunited, the little family walked sedately toward a nearby creek and waded in, the little ones bobbing on the current as if they didn't have a care in the world. I glanced at my little panty-net lady and she grabbed my arm and squeezed it and smiled up at me with tears in her eyes. I hugged her back, grinning from ear to ear.

14. Please Don't Play with Wild Animals

When I cleared my duck call, dispatch sent me to pick up a bat that had been found in an apartment complex. In general bats are good to have around. They are quiet and unobtrusive, eating mosquitoes and other insects by night and sleeping by day. Unfortunately, they are also our main rabies carriers, so we're on alert when we get a bat call.

When I arrived a group of teens met me at the door. Three girls and three guys invited me in and pointed to a backpack in the middle of the room.

"He's in there," one of the girls said.

"Did any of you touch it?" I asked.

"You guys touched it right?" she said, looking at the guys. They looked at me with guilty expressions and one of them quickly said, "No, we didn't touch it." I knew I would need to test the bat, just to be on the safe side.

"How did you get it in the backpack?" I asked.

"We just held it open next to it and the bat crawled in," one of the girls said.

That sounded legitimate as bats are attracted to small, dark places. I put on my leather gloves and used the lid of my clear plastic "critter carrier" to scoop him out of the backpack and into the container. I held him up and looked closely at him.

Bats are fascinating little creatures. Tiny beady eyes stared brightly back at me as the velvety brown body gave way to soft skin-like wings with tiny climbing hooks on the ends. I took all of the kids' information, sad that the bat would have to be sacrificed for the rabies test. The only way to test bats for rabies is to examine the brain.

I recalled a previous case where someone had brought in a baby opossum that had bitten a child. We told them we would test the animal for rabies, though opossums are almost never carriers. A few days later the father called and asked me for the test results. "Oh, you don't have to worry, they were negative," I told him. "Oh, good," came his reply. "We would like to pick him up and release him back in the woods." There was a moment of silence as I struggled over how to inform him the animal had to have its brain removed for the test. For a second I even considered just giving them back the brainless body. Opossums with a brain act a lot like opossums without a brain. They just don't do a whole lot and they frequently play dead anyway. Realizing I had to come clean, I informed the disappointed caller of the opossum's unfortunate demise.

I had, at one time, done all of the brain removals for rabies testing in the county. Strange but necessary work, it paid a premium and if I was going to have to be away from my kids every day I might as well get some extra pay for the icky stuff. The first time I saw an opossum's brain things became much clearer. It's astonishing to see the difference of the brain of an opossum and any other mammal of the same size. The other animals have a walnut-sized brain that looks like a human brain, all convoluted and seamed. The opossum brain, however, looks the brain stem of the other animals. It's small and smooth, strictly the basics, enough to handle breathing, chewing, and wandering in front of cars. It's like the old joke: Why did the chicken cross the road? Answer: To prove to the opossum that it could be done.

I took the bat into the shelter, sent it to the lab, and thought no more about it until a few days later when a supervisor approached me in the hall at the office. "Your bat from Bell Creek just came back positive. What kind of exposure did we have?"

Stunned, I flashed back to the memory of the kids with the bat. What if they had been exposed? I remembered the little beady eyes staring at me. I distinctly remembered that he had appeared perfectly healthy. I explained my concerns about the teens and he went off to make some phone calls. Bummer. Thankfully, after some careful questioning by the parents, it was determined that the teens had not touched the bat and so had no exposure to rabies. Their guilty expressions came from harassing the little creature during the capture.

I was discussing the bat situation over lunch in the break room with Angie, a woman who works in the front office, when one of the newly hired clerks walked in. Brenda seemed like a pleasant young woman and we invited her to join us. It was payday and Brenda mentioned she had to hand over her paycheck to her husband as soon as she got it. Angie and I were incensed. What kind of controlling Neanderthal demanded his wife's paycheck? We jumped in and advised her that she could take her check to the bank and open her own account if she wanted. She thought about it for a moment, then seemed to make a sudden decision. "You're right," she declared. "I should have some say in what I do with my own money. I'm going to go open an account right now." She got up and headed for her car with a new sense of purpose. Angie and I continued our conversation, happy that we had empowered a young woman in a controlling marriage.

Brenda returned half an hour later with a smile. "Thanks to you, I now have my own bank account in my own name." She headed toward the front office, leaving me and Angie to exchange satisfied glances, then she turned and added, "And he can't say anything about it because I haven't gambled in almost two months." She continued on her way as our faces fell. "Oh, I suck," I wailed, the moment she was out of earshot. "I can't believe we just did that. I should just mind my own friggin business!" I buried my head in my hands as Angie added, "Her poor husband is probably doing everything he can to pay the bills with a gambling addicted wife and we go and butt in."

We never did find out if Brenda beat her gambling problem because a few days later she counted her drawer at the end of the day and it was ten dollars over. "Awesome," she said, holding up a ten dollar bill. "I've got ten bucks." She slipped the bill into her purse, much to the shock of the other clerks. Brenda seemed confused when the supervisor came out a few moments later and advised her they wouldn't need her services any longer.

15. I Should Have Been a Coal Miner

Not everyone thrives on animal control work. You have to be able to get a lot of mileage out of one good rescue or one satisfied customer. And we have some pretty rough days out there. Of course, some days everything goes right, your rescues are successful, you get your cows back in the field, catch your loose dogs, and even the people you cite are pleasant. Today was not that day.

It started at 2:30 a.m. with an owner arrest on the far side of the county. The woman left the bar at closing time with her dog in the car and was arrested for a DUI on her way home. I arrived on the scene to find a Highway Patrol officer and a tow truck driver seated by the side of the road where they'd waited for the hour it took me to wake up, get my tired butt dressed, yank my hair into a ponytail and drive the distance in the dark. The woman was sitting in the back of the patrol car, handcuffed and crying, begging me to take good care of her dog, Lady, a Rottweiler. Jeez, I thought, if she would have rolled another hundred yards she would have been in the next county and their Highway Patrol and animal control could have dealt with it.

By the time I loaded Lady in the truck, drove to the shelter, impounded her and drove home it was nearly 5:00 a.m. and too late to go back to bed. So I fed the animals, folded some laundry and packed the kids' lunches before leaving for work. On my way in I remembered I had court that day for a horse neglect case, so I drove to the courthouse and waited for hours in the hall because I couldn't be in the courtroom when other witnesses were testifying. I never was called and the case was thrown out in spite of the horse dying a miserable death due to lack of care. I had spent many hours investigating the case, put together a heck of a report and all for nothing. I felt discouraged as I headed out to handle my calls, way behind already.

The day continued to go downhill. I ended up in the middle of a gang dispute involving some pit bulls and was in fear for my life when the police showed up. Next I was screamed and cursed at by a platinum blonde in a BMW because I cited her for her Labradoodles license. I picked up a dead cat in the road that smelled so bad and was so maggoty I gagged and had the dry heaves as I shoveled it into a bag. I had forgotten to get lunch and felt lightheaded but had lost my appetite. I forced myself to eat some nuts I kept in my truck, all the while thinking I was probably the one who was nuts. Next I had a call to pick up an injured kitten and hurried back to the clinic, but it died on the way. When I got to work and checked my email there was a message from one of the adopters of a puppy I had fostered, saying she had just been dumped by her fiancé and needed to find a new home for the dog.

Paul was away for a week working and he called in the late afternoon, which cheered me temporarily, but then I just got to missing him terribly and was really in a funk. By the time I finished my paperwork and impounds it was late and I still needed to fuel up my truck on the way home since I was on call again for the night. At the pumps I got a whiff of something foul and realized I hadn't disposed of the dead cat and it was stinking up the back of my truck. I was overtired and stressed and just wanted to bawl but it wouldn't do any good without Paul there to hold me, so I sucked it up and headed home.

As I drove, the situation of the dead cat reminded me of an animal control officer I knew from another county who finally left the business. A stunning, green-eyed blonde with an impressive set of store-bought boobs, Marina seemed out of place in a dog truck. Still, she did a good job, even after snapping off most of her perfectly manicured nails in a wrestling match with a loose pig. She had her share of icky calls, but she rarely complained, and then one day she quit out of the blue, not even giving two weeks' notice.

I ran into Marina months after she left the animal control business, and I took a break to go for coffee to catch up. She was wearing a stylish, low-cut blouse and a short skirt with heels. There was not a dog hair in sight. I tried to brush off my uniform, which was spotted with nameless hairs, dog slobber and a little bit of cow crap from a call at a dairy. We sat down with our drinks, and I asked her why she had left.

Marina studied her coffee cup for a moment and then sighed and ran her once again perfect nails through her hair. "I was picking up a dead duck on Skywing Drive and I had to block traffic with my truck to get it. The thing had been there a while and it was completely disgusting and nasty. I grabbed a leg with my glove and just then this gorgeous hunk of a man who was stopped behind me in his Porsche walked up to see if I needed any help."

I could easily picture any red-blooded male jumping at the chance to help Marina with anything. She took a gulp of coffee and continued. "He really couldn't see what I was doing, so I tried to swing the thing into the truck really fast, but the leg came off in my hand and the rotted, maggoty carcass flopped at his feet, splattering his pants with some disgusting juice. He took one look at me with a duck leg in my hand, then at his pants and the duck lying in the street and turned kind of green. He got the dry heaves and started staggering around the roadway, gagging in front of everyone who was stopped. I apologized profusely and offered to get his pants cleaned but he just gagged some more and stumbled back to his car." She looked into my eyes with her thick, dark lashes. "And that was the day I quit."

Marina told me she was working as a legal aide in an office now and she loved it. She leaned forward earnestly. "It was pure luck that I got this job. I

85

had no experience when I interviewed. I can't believe they hired me."

I averted my eyes as her position offered a spectacular view of her barely restrained investments. "Really?" I said. "You must have made a great impression." But I was happy for her, and her bosses seemed to be getting their money's worth.

The memory of Marina and the dead duck made me laugh out loud and I felt a little better, but I still questioned my employment. Why did I choose to subject myself to daily abuse and witness so much neglect and cruelty? Why couldn't I have chosen something easier and more rewarding like tax collecting or coal mining?

I pulled into my driveway and found that Nikki had made dinner, Shay had set the table, and they had even put flowers in a vase and a lit a pair of candles. We all sat down to dinner and I was starting to feel better when my cell phone rang. I was so exhausted and glad to be home that I could have screamed, but I called in and got a report of a woman whose kitten was stuck behind some sort of entertainment center in her home.

Hoping I could talk her through it, I phoned the distraught woman. I asked her why she didn't just move the furniture and she said it was too tall and attached to the wall. After further questioning I decided I had better check it out and I told her I was on my way. I grabbed a drill and some other things I might need. As I headed out, Nikki asked to come along.

It was good to spend time with Nik, just chatting about our day and hearing the latest updates on school and her friends as I drove. When we arrived, Ms. Belinski, a plumpish widow in her sixties, answered the door and escorted us into her cozy condo. We were also greeted by her darling elderly pit bull, Minnie. Minnie was fawn and white with the sweetest big brown eyes I had ever seen. Her tail wagged eagerly as Nikki and I stroked her faded muzzle. After soaking up the attention for a moment, Minnie turned and walked to the entertainment center, anxiously gazing at it while whining and wagging her tail. "Minnie has been so upset since Buffy's been stuck," said Ms. Belinski. "She won't come away from there for more than a moment. She and Buffy are best friends. They are my only companions since my husband died."

Looking at the towering piece of furniture I could see the problem was bigger than I thought. The thing was about seven feet high, built into the corner and attached securely to the walls. There was no moving that sucker. Add to that, it almost reached the ceiling so I couldn't even climb up and see behind it as there wasn't room. I couldn't imagine how the silly cat could have gotten up there and fallen down the narrow space behind the unit. For some reason the thing had been built with this gap behind it where the cat was stuck, but there was no way to lower cat grabbers or anything else back there.

The cabinet shelves were filled with fragile knickknacks and I was amused to see they were all glued to the wood. Ms. Belinski saw my grin and said "I glued them down so Buffy can't knock them over."

I could hear the cat clawing around in the narrow space behind the unit. Minnie cocked her head curiously at the noise. I dreaded cutting a hole in this beautiful custom piece of furniture but there didn't seem to be any other way. Ms. Belinski was more than willing for me to cut into it, but I brainstormed for a moment, hoping for another solution.

Just then a scrambling sound came from behind as the cat again attempted to climb up, but she didn't make it more than a foot or so before sliding back down. "How about a rope, Mom?" Nikki asked, as she stroked Minnie's broad head. A rope was a long shot. Not many cats would climb straight up a rope, but I would try everything before destroying some furniture. I sent her to the truck for a rope.

Meanwhile, Ms. Belinski produced a high step stool. I nudged Minnie aside and climbed to the top before asking Nik to pass me the thick cotton rope. I lowered the end down the hole and immediately heard frantic scrambling up the side. Minnie's broad head followed the sound upward as the kitten made progress, clawing her way up the rope. Minnie gave a couple of woofs of encouragement. Within twenty seconds the ruffled kitty scrambled out the top. I took her in my hands and placed her, purring, into her owner's arms.

Ms. Belinski cried as she hugged Buffy close to her and thanked us over and over. Nikki gave me a high five and Minnie's whines turned high-pitched with joy as she jumped up to sniff her buddy. Her tail beat a fast tempo.

As Nikki and I drove home chatting excitedly about the call, it occurred to me I had the best job in the world. I had made someone's day, spent quality time with my daughter, rescued an animal in need, and been paid for it. It doesn't get much better than that. Marina can have her store-bought boobs and cushy office.

16. Paul's Coming Home!

I hummed to myself as I tossed the salad and peeked into the oven at the roasting potatoes. Paul had been working overseas for several weeks and would be home any minute. I could hardly wait to see him. Scott was camping with some buddies and Nikki and Shay were staying overnight with friends after a school event. Even our housemate and dear friend, Mickey, was away, house-sitting for an acquaintance. Except for the dogs and cats that snoozed on every available surface, I had the place to myself. I had tried desperately to get someone to take my on-call shift for the night, but no one was available. I hoped it would be quiet like it had been for the last three nights. I ran a brush through my hair, still damp from a shower and spritzed on some perfume.

As I set the table and lit some candles I saw Luci's ears perk up. I heard the sound of Paul's car door slam and ran to the front door to meet him. His face lit up when he saw me and he dropped his suitcase and wrapped me in a bear hug as the dogs crowded around, sniffing and wagging. I breathed in his delicious scent, my face buried in his neck, arms wrapped around him. Wow, it's been a long time. He kissed me tenderly and leaned back to look into my eyes. "I've missed you so much," he said, kissing me again. "How are you?"

We held hands as we ate dinner, talking and laughing, our feet intertwined under the table. It was fun catching up on Paul's travels and my work and what the kids had been up to. Now and then he would stop and smile at me and give that look, the same look he's been giving me for more than twenty years, the one that makes my heart do a flip-flop. He's got these gorgeous green eyes I find irresistible and his hand felt warm and wonderful in mine. I felt a tingle of anticipation and wondered how we had been so blessed with such a loving and passionate marriage. After dinner Paul took a quick shower and I put the leftovers away. The dishes could wait.

I slipped on a silky nightgown and climbed into bed with my book, only half paying attention to the story as Paul brushed his teeth and then tapped the toothbrush against the sink before putting it away. The book fell to the floor as he climbed in next to me and pulled me close. "I love you so much," he said. "I'm sorry I had to be gone so long."

"It's okay, you're here now," I whispered.

It was bliss just holding him. He kissed my face and eyelids and my mouth. Oh, this is the best, I thought, feeling overwhelmed by desire as our bodies melted together.

Just then, the cheery beat of my cell phone interrupted our embrace. Seriously! Surely not now! Not after three weeks away from home! Not after three nights without a single call out! Maybe it wouldn't be anything serious. Maybe I could talk someone through their issue and go back to sucking the lips off my husband!

I lunged across Paul to grab the phone from the nightstand. "Hello?" I said, a little breathlessly.

"Hi, this is John in sheriff's dispatch. We've got a dog attack for you, with the dog still at large and deputies en route. We need you out there as soon as possible." He went on as I scribbled the victim's address on a scrap of paper.

Damn! I leapt out of bed and started yanking on my clothes as Paul groaned and pulled a pillow over his head. "I'm so sorry, sweetie." I pushed the pillow aside and kissed his cheek. "I'll be back."

"I'll be waiting," he murmured, from under his pillow.

I roared out of the driveway, glancing at the map book as I went. My mind flashed back to Paul and I shook my head to clear it. I had to pay attention or I would miss my turn in the dark.

Twenty minutes later I was pulling up to the victim's home. Could it be true? My dog attack turned out to be a couple of punctures to the thumb by a ten-pound Chihuahua. The victim, a burly, bearded, tattooed biker-type, seemed totally traumatized. What a baby! I was the one who should be traumatized, leaving my husband in the middle of a passionate embrace. But I had to feel sorry for the guy. He was trying to catch the little stray dog and it never occurred to him it would bite. He felt terrible and even worse when told the dog would be quarantined for ten days. I took a report and advised him to avoid grabbing scared dogs on the street in the future, no matter how little they are. It took another twenty minutes to corner and capture the terrified dog. I made him cozy with a blanket in my truck and headed out.

Later, tiptoeing into our room I gazed at my sleeping husband. I had a feeling he would be waking up soon.

17. You Are a Stud

The place was swarming with police and SWAT guys when I pulled in. They were all big powerful men and they looked at me in dismay when I got out of my truck. I'm pretty used to that response when I arrive on calls that might be dangerous or take some muscle. I'm 5'8" and weigh around 140 pounds, and with my blonde ponytail I've been called Barbie more than once. I could see these men were hoping for a couple of big guys.

One of the officers, a brawny six-footer, stepped up to fill me in on the situation. "Everyone who lives here has been arrested. A pit bull confined to the garage is extremely aggressive. When I attempted to enter he tried to attack me. I barely slammed the door in time." He paused, nervously. "So how do you want to do this?"

"Let me take a look and see what we have."

I grabbed a catch pole out of the truck and followed him into the rundown house. He pointed to a door in the kitchen that led to the garage. I cracked it cautiously and peered inside. A roar erupted from within and I caught a glimpse of a dark blur as a mass of muscle and snarling teeth hit the door with a mighty crash, jarring my shoulder as I braced against it.

I took a deep breath. "I'm going to go in to try to get my pole on him. Hold the door cracked enough to see me, but don't do anything unless the dog gets a hold of me. If that happens, shoot." I was a little worried about shooting in that confined space with the concrete floor posing a ricochet hazard. My master plan was to not let the dog get a hold of me.

The officer looked at me in shock. "Let me get this straight. You're going in there alone?"

"I haven't had one eat me yet," I replied, thinking, there's a first time for everything.

The man looked at me like I was completely nuts, which could be a possibility. Still, there's some thrill in the challenge of accomplishing a goal with the least possible trauma to human and animal. The dog was likely acting in fear, and I felt fairly confident I could get him out safely. Worst case scenario, I get a nasty bite and the officer has to shoot the dog to prevent further injury to me and others. The worst, worst case scenario involves my getting attacked and the officer missing the dog and shooting me. I tried not to think about it.

Sometimes I get lucky and can noose a dog through a doorway without even entering the room, so I eased the door open just enough to get my catch pole through the opening. The snarling rose in pitch as I squinted in the dim light, trying to get the noose over the dog's head. The dog backed away, eyes blazing, still growling, as I eased the pole toward him. Even the most ferocious dog will usually back down if you keep coming toward it, so I entered the room slowly, pulling the door almost closed, and asked the officer to hold the door. "If he dodges past me toward the door just close it," I called to him.

"With you inside?!"

"I don't want him to slip past you. I'll holler if I need you."

"You've got to be kidding!" He clearly had serious doubts about my dog-wrestling ability and seemed to be expecting to witness his first fatal dog mauling. In the room now with the dog, I waited for my eyes to adjust. It was a cluttered one-car garage. I looked around for a light switch but couldn't see one.

There was only one small dusty window, and the mid-afternoon light coming in was dim.

As I slowly approached the dog, he backed into the corner, snarling horribly, every tooth bared, eyes dilated to nothing but big black pupils. He wasn't buying my happy talk. A pool of strong-smelling urine formed beneath him, revealing his terror as I eased quietly forward, finally slipping the noose over his snarling face and carefully cinching it to a safe level. At that, the dog launched straight up the wall, crashing into a pile of boxes and knocking a row of storage shelves to the floor with a tremendous crash. It probably sounded a lot worse than it was, and I couldn't blame the dog. He must have been terrified with a bunch of strangers in his house. I saw the officer peer around the door, gun drawn. I smiled encouragingly and attempted to give a thumbs-up while still holding the snarling, fighting animal on the end of my pole.

At last, I managed to rein the dog in. "Let's go, buddy," I said, softly, leading him toward the door. The officer held the door open with the tips of his fingers while standing back and out of my way as far as possible. The dog continued to growl, but came along without a struggle as the group of officers parted to let me pass through. With one hand, I held the pole while pulling my truck ramp down with the other. I used both hands to guide the dog up the ramp and into the truck. I could see the dog's entire demeanor change once I got him out of the house. "You're gonna be okay, buddy" I said, scratching him behind the ears. I got the tiniest twitch of the tucked tail before I slipped the catch pole noose off him and closed and locked the door. Then I took my first breath in about three minutes. It had gone as smoothly as it could have gone.

An officer walked up and slapped me on the back. "Nicely done!" All the officers seemed a lot more cheerful as they thanked me and returned to finishing up their investigation.

I climbed into my truck and was starting it up when another officer approached me. He looked me squarely in the eyes. "YOU," he said, pausing for emphasis, "are a STUD." Then he turned and walked away.

A stud is not what I strive to be, but coming from one of those guys it

94

was a big compliment. They face off with armed criminals who could kill them and don't even bat an eye. When it comes to the dogs, though, they seem certain they'll be annihilated. I'll take the dogs over the bad guys any day. At least dogs show what they're feeling. They don't act nice while plotting to kill you.

18. The Things We See

The old man's eyes were closed and he lay back on his bed with his head on the pillow and the covers tucked up to his chest. Even the wispy white hair on his head looked unruffled. His arms were wrapped around his little blond Chihuahua, "Chiquita," who looked at me quietly from her spot snuggled against her beloved person. For a Chihuahua to fail to bark when a stranger enters the house is a miracle in itself. The only way it could have been a more peaceful scene would have been if the man had not been dead.

The man lived alone in a senior housing apartment and management had been alerted when he failed to pick up his morning paper. The police officer had found him just as I had, reached in next to the little dog to check for a pulse and contacted the coroner's office and animal control. We're usually the first ones on the scene when a body is discovered if animals are present. The police and coroners don't want to have to worry about the pets as they do their investigation and remove the body.

In this case, the man's son waited downstairs to claim his father's dog but didn't want to come up to the room. My only duty was to transport the dog to the lobby. I gently scooped the unresisting Chiquita from her place in the man's arms and cuddled her to my chest.

When I arrived in the lobby I looked around, unsure who I was supposed to be handing off the dog to. A man walked into the lobby and made his way toward me. He looked younger than I expected, probably in his forties, with fair hair and a handsome face streaked with tears, but the family resemblance was there. He reached for Chiquita and burst into sobs as he held her. I put an arm around him and he leaned in for a moment and hugged me before taking a deep breath and composing himself. "Thank you," he said. "I'm so glad to at least have her." He glanced at the small bundle in his arms and turned and walked away.

Some of my coworkers hate doing coroner's cases, but I don't usually mind them. I hate to see anyone suffering, but most of my coroner's cases have been very peaceful. The deceased have often been like Chiquita's owner, elderly, and passed away quietly at home, surrounded by their pets. I want to be able to gently provide for their beloved companions in a way that I would want my pets to be handled after my death. Of course, some cases have been ugly, traumatic crime scenes or suicides or even bodies that have decomposed or been fed upon by desperate and starving pets. Those can have a lasting effect on everyone involved, but the animals still need to be removed and cared for, so we do it.

One of my first coroner's cases was a 98-year-old woman named Fern Gilbert. I parked the dog truck in her driveway and could hear the police officers talking near the back of the property, so I went around behind the house and greeted them. They were standing near a sheep shed. They said hello and then began advising me about what animals were on the property. The sheep bleated loudly and I had to step a little closer to hear what the officer was saying. I nearly tripped over something and glanced down at my feet at what appeared to be a little Halloween prop only to realize it was the tiny and very much deceased Ms. Gilbert lying among some debris in front of the sheep shed. Startled, I leapt back, much to the amusement of the officers.

It took a moment to compose myself. I had assumed the old lady was in the house. I mean, for heaven's sakes, she was ninety-eight years old. I hadn't expected her to be out be-bopping around back by herself. I had kind of pictured her in a wheelchair in the living room watching reruns of Lawrence Welk with a live-in nurse when she passed. By now I know that in this job you can never assume anything.

After I pulled it together, I spent an hour or so organizing care and transport for the animals on the property. There were sheep, some ducks, a small dog and several cats. Fern had never had children, but I finally reached her next of kin, a niece named Katherine Albright, by phone. Katherine knew someone who would take the sheep and ducks. Katherine herself agreed to take the cats and she asked that I find a home for little Mick, Fern's Dachshund.

I made Mick a cozy bed in my truck and then took a last look around the place to make sure I hadn't missed any animals. As I wandered around, I got to thinking about Fern. The officers told me she had lived alone and independently and still drove her old pickup truck. Apparently, she had been out feeding the sheep when she succumbed to what was likely a heart attack. The mail carrier had called for a welfare check when her mail had not been collected.

It fascinated me to know the woman was in such good health right until the end. No one was spoon-feeding her in a hospital bed, there were no tubes, no needles, just Fern puttering around her one-acre city lot until the last moment. The zoning department had even ignored the fact that she had sheep in the city. After all, her place had been out in the country when she moved there in 1942. The city had grown up around her.

Neighbors who had stopped in said she was as sharp as a tack until the end, too, although some interesting quirks in her character were beginning to reveal themselves as I wandered the property. She seemed to have a strong fear of running out of water because everywhere I walked were jugs and bottles filled with water. Old milk jugs and wine bottles, quart jars and soda containers had been pressed into service as water receptacles and were stacked everywhere on the property. Many of them did not have lids and were green with algae. The mosquitoes were having a field day.

Inside the house were more surprises. It appeared that she had never thrown anything away, ever. It was the home of a classic hoarder. At least it was things she hoarded, and not large numbers of animals. I could see that the house was a once-spacious three-bedroom that over the years Fern had stuffed to the gills. A police officer and I worked my way around the house looking for animals and were stunned by the amount of clutter. This was not a simple case of too many knickknacks. The bedrooms were filled floor to ceiling with clothes, boxes, magazines and every other imaginable item. There was literally no way to enter the rooms; they were a solid wall of stuff. A small bed had been made on an enclosed porch and it appeared that Fern slept there. There was no other available surface. The hallways were lined and stacked higher than my head with things as well, leaving just a narrow path that wound through to the back door. Anyone any bigger than me would have had trouble squeezing through. My hips brushed against the stacks as I passed by. I found no sign of other animals, and sweet little Mick was adopted within a week or so.

I drove by Fern's house occasionally after that for some months. The place stood untouched. I wondered if her family was trying to get up the nerve to go through all that stuff. It was overwhelming just to think about. It could take years to do it. Then one day I drove by and everything was gone, even the house. Some dumpsters sat on the property, but every scrap of the house and the other debris was gone. It was just a clean, bare lot. I doubt they even sorted through the stuff, they just brought in a huge tractor and scooped everything into them. Whatever valuables were in there, they must have figured, probably wouldn't have been worth having to pick through all that stuff to find. Several months later I saw a brand new house on the lot and a beautifully landscaped yard. Nothing remained of nearly a century of saving everything.

Coroner's cases are often intriguing. One of my coworkers has commented on how often his coroner's cases have been nude when he has arrived. His theory is that when they start feeling ill they get up and want to change clothes so they'll look nice for the paramedics but pass away before they

99

can finish. There may be something to it, as several times I have arrived on a coroner's scene to find a completely nude deceased person in the home. One elderly man was dead on the floor in a doorway and I had to step over his naked body to access the rooms in the house. He owned multiple snakes and I was taking them out to the truck in their terrariums. It was somewhat unnerving to have to worry about tripping over old Harold every time I came and went. Besides that, he was flat on his back and it seemed he was completely missing a certain organ. I didn't want to stare but I was puzzled. I glanced down again as I stepped over him and realized it was there, it was just sort of … deflated. Like a balloon with the air out of it. What the heck? Is that what happens when they get old? Was it lack of use? Or just because he was dead? The coroner arrived then and I wanted to ask her about it, but somehow I just couldn't bring myself to do it.

The coroner wasn't at all what I expected. An attractive and engaging redhead of maybe forty-five years old, she was stylishly dressed in a skirt and heels. She chatted with me cheerfully as she helped me carry out the larger snake cages, maneuvering expertly over Harold as she balanced her end of the cage. I finally asked her how she had gotten involved in her line of work. She told me she had always been fascinated with the human body and considered becoming a doctor but didn't want to have to worry about making a fatal mistake. As a coroner she could solve mysteries and crimes without having a person's life in her hands. Even if she were only verifying that a person died a natural death it was a comfort to the families.

In sharp contrast to the coroner were the two guys who came to load up the bodies for transport. These pale, skinny young men could barely put two words together. I pictured them sitting in the basement at the morgue playing dungeons and dragons, surrounded by dead bodies.

My coworker, Jim, once responded to a coroner's case and walked into a nightmare scene. The woman had apparently been dead for several weeks before she was found and was in an advanced state of decomposition. The odor was indescribable. There's nothing quite like the stench of death, but more

100

horrifying was the situation with the animals. Two sweet, apricot Miniature Poodles and a tabby cat were locked in the house with the poor dead woman and had nothing to eat, so you can imagine the consequences. The whole picture was overwhelming and the pets carried the terrible odor on their coats. Jim had the dry heaves and kept gagging as he carried the animals out to his truck. It was months before he stopped dreaming about the scene.

Meanwhile, the outraged family demanded the bloodthirsty creatures be euthanized for what they had done. I really wanted to ask them why in the world no one had bothered to call and check on their elderly mother for at least two weeks, but I didn't. The shelter supervisor told them the euthanasia request was unreasonable for healthy, adoptable animals and we were able to find homes for all three of them after a thorough grooming.

When a coroner's cases involve a murder, we have to be very careful not to disturb the scene as sometimes the animals are integral to the case. Once I picked up a large blue and gold macaw from the scene of a murder. The killing was unsolved and I spent a lot of time listening to the bird's chatter for clues but never heard anything conclusive and he was eventually sent to a bird rescue facility.

Usually a law enforcement agency discovers a body and then calls animal control, so I was surprised to get a request from the coroner's office itself one evening around dusk. They asked that I pick up a deceased dog from the morgue. I wondered about it all the way there. When I arrived, Ben, the guy on duty, informed me that the dog's owner had also been killed and Ben couldn't bear to leave the dog's body behind when he picked her up. I asked him what happened and he explained that the deceased had been in a minor fender bender on the freeway during rush hour traffic. She and the other driver had pulled to the side and when she opened the door to speak to the other driver, her dog had darted out into traffic. She had dashed after the dog and both were struck and killed instantly.

I was horrified by the story and asked if the deceased's family had been informed. I was told they hadn't yet been able to reach anyone. Beyond the open

101

door a bulky body bag lay on a gurney. A smaller one was tucked in beside it. Ben handed me the dog owner's drivers license so I could get her information for the impound (we always make a record of any animal we pick up, dead or alive) and I paused a moment looking at her photo. She was an attractive middle-aged woman with a sweet smile and neatly styled frosted hair. Life is so weird, I thought. One minute you're headed home from a few errands with your dog and the next you're both lying on a slab in black plastic bags.

I loaded up the smaller bag, feeling the still-supple form inside, and headed back the shelter. Someone's world was about to cave in. I saw from the woman's birthdate that she was in her early fifties, and I hoped that if she had kids they weren't still at home. I was haunted by the thought of a husband pacing around, wondering why in the world his wife was so late.

At the shelter I removed the cumbersome bag and surveyed the dog sadly. He was a well-groomed poodle and the little body was surprisingly unblemished. He wore a license, and I punched the number into the computer and viewed his information. He was Sam, four years old, current on license and listed to the woman in the accident. I changed his status to "dead" to prevent the family from getting a painful renewal notice in the mail and I wrapped the body in a clean flower-print sheet and placed it in the cooler. I later learned he was cremated and buried with his owner.

19. Animal Hoarders

Another of my coroner's cases came on a Saturday afternoon as I was headed back to the shelter after a busy day of work. I detoured to the address I was given and pulled up behind a patrol car parked in front of a small studio. A young, dark-haired police officer was sitting in his vehicle. He looked shattered and pale. By the look on his face I was expecting a really bad scene, maybe a grisly murder or a suicide. Or maybe he was just new to the job, because when I entered the tiny, cluttered home there was just a little elderly woman dead in her bed where she had apparently passed away in her sleep. Granted, the place was a mess and the ammonia smell was pretty strong, biting my nostrils as I entered, but I'd seen worse. A cat bolted under the bed, but still it was a quiet scene. The woman's eyes were peacefully closed and her two little dogs were sat next to her peering at me anxiously. The dogs looked like Yorkshire Terrier mixes, probably weighed about 10 pounds each and were tan with sweet whiskery faces. I made happy talk to them as I reached for them but they jumped over and around the body skittishly a few times before I was able to scoop them up and carry them to my truck.

I went back inside for the cat and looked around. The whole place was just one room with a bathroom and closet at one end and the single bed against the wall to one side. There was endless clutter and feces mixed in with clothes and garbage on the floor. I felt a little creepy crawling on the filthy floor under the bed for the cat but was able to get her and put her into a carrier. I spotted another cat, and then several more hiding in every available space. I began to carefully gather up cats from where they hid among the chaos of the room. Each time I thought I had the last cat, I would see another. Final count: eleven cats. No wonder the place reeked of ammonia. Strangely, there was no litter box and no cat door to the outside. It appeared the animals never left the house. I saw that the little bathroom was completely inaccessible as well. It was piled high with clothes, pet carriers and other odds and ends. I didn't even want to know where the resident had relieved herself. It didn't make any sense. As I walked back and forth carrying the pets to the truck something began niggling at the back of my mind.

I walked over to the deceased woman in the bed and bent down and looked directly into her still face. And it hit me. Betty Binkly! I hadn't seen Betty in a year or so, but there was no doubt it was her. Betty and I went way back, though I didn't recognize her at first, without her middle finger up. Long before I worked for animal control I had worked in a vet clinic nearby and Betty often came in seeking care for one of her many pets. She was a tiny woman who dressed in endless layers of ragged clothing. She rarely had any money and was so crazy and smelled so bad we had to air the place out after one of her visits. The vets certainly never made any profit from her, and she was such a difficult client the only reason they saw her at all was out of compassion for her pets. When I worked at the shelter I learned she was one of our county's most notorious animal hoarders. Betty's relationship with animal control went back at least twenty years. At one time she had squatted in a travel trailer without plumbing in a wooded area not far from the shelter. She had around twenty dogs and forty or fifty cats when our department was first called in to investigate. Officers found that along with the dogs and cats she had a fully grown buck goat living with her in her filthy trailer. The goat's name was Ned Binkly and Betty called him her husband.

Does and baby goat kids are among the most charming of creatures. A neutered male goat, called a wether, can make a wonderful pet, but a whiff of an un-neutered buck in a distant farmyard is enough to make me want to avoid the place altogether. It's a strong, rank odor that can assault the senses from great distances. The thought of living inside a small travel trailer with that stench was mind-boggling.

Years ago, officers had confiscated all the animals and taken Betty to court because of their terrible health and living conditions. She had cursed out the judge heartily and he had given her probation and forbidden her to own animals for three years. Eighteen months later officers removed seven dogs and sixteen cats from the property. Betty was again taken to court. On the way home she stopped at the store for hot dogs and acquired two kittens that were being given away in front of the supermarket. Of course, the kittens grew up and had litters, and Betty kept grabbing every stray or free pet she could find. Over the years the area was developed, she was evicted from the trailer, and we were again called to pick up large numbers of animals over her vehement protests. She had moved several times after that and we lost track of where she was living, although we sometimes saw her walking around town. When she saw one of our trucks she would shake her fist violently at us, or worse, flip us the bird with an arthritic finger and shout curses, causing people to stop and stare. Other times she waved eagerly like a long lost friend and flagged us down for a pleasant chat about her latest pets that she wasn't supposed to have anyway.

Betty must have been in her late seventies by the time she died. Maybe she had mellowed. We'd had fewer problems with her in the last year or so. It could be she simply wasn't able to get out and gather animals as much at her age. And despite the mess and odor the two dogs and multiple cats she had at the end were neutered and in good health.

Another elderly woman, I later learned, had taken Betty under her wing and helped her toward the end. She was probably responsible for the fact the animals were in better shape than usual. Elizabeth Blalock was a wealthy widow who had stopped once to give Betty a ride to the vet in her BMW when she saw Betty hobbling down the street with a cat in a carrier. Elizabeth was like the anti-Betty, beautiful and elegant in her old age. She was gracious and kind and would help anyone in need.

Elizabeth owned a pampered Dachshund named Charles that went everywhere with her. She had taken to stopping by Betty's hovel every week to bring her groceries and pet food. She gave her rides to the vet and paid her bills. She had even tried to arrange for her housekeeper to come in and clean Betty's place, but the poor woman had taken one look inside and declared there wasn't enough money in the world to entice her to even attempt to tackle that mess.

When Elizabeth heard of Betty's passing she came to the shelter and picked up the two little dogs for a friend who wanted to adopt them. She networked extensively and relentlessly encouraged her friends to open their beautiful, spacious homes to Betty's cats, who were soon adopted into lives of luxury. When the last cat went to its new home, I breathed a sigh of relief. It was an end of an era.

Hoarding is a serious mental disorder often marked by keeping more animals than a person can reasonably care for. Rather than deliberate cruelty, it's the inability to recognize they are harming their pets by their lack of care. Betty was probably our most memorable and visible hoarder, but several others have made an impression as well. One woman had multiple horses and I know from experience that the price of feeding even one horse is not for the faint of heart. This wise woman, Claudia Lynchman, came up with a perfect solution. Instead of pricy alfalfa and grain she fed them stale bread and moldy produce she got for free from behind the local grocery stores. I was new to the job and fairly naive the first time I went to her rundown place and viewed the feed pans full of the day's haul. I stared in horror at the moldy Brussels sprouts and ever-so-nutritious stale hot dog buns that lay untouched on the bottom of the buckets. If I had ever let one of my pampered horses so much as take a nibble of that mess they would have gotten colic and died on the spot.

Glancing around Claudia's property, I found a morbid fascination in the sheer chaos of the place. Claudia would sit in the back of her old pickup truck full of bread and take the plastic bags off the loaves and toss them aside. Over the years the entire place was practically paved in old bags with a few hearty weeds poking up between them. Bags in the water trough shared space with the algae and bags nestled among the endless debris spread everywhere. There were bags piled up against the fences and bags snagged on the barbed wire. The bags on the barbed wire had an unintended function: they made the dangerous barbs more visible to the horses.

The surprising thing about Claudia's five horses was they didn't look that terrible. They were of acceptable weight and appeared fairly healthy. Some were in a pasture together, but others were in paddocks too small for long-term living, but since the horses were able to move around a little they weren't technically a violation of the law. She didn't have a farrier but her horses must have had really good feet because they seemed to just chip off at an acceptable length. Not perfect, but again, not a violation of the law that we could really enforce.

Our department had attempted to force Claudia to improve the horse's conditions in the past but she would just stare blankly into space and deny there was a problem. Officers had even taken her to court a few years prior and gotten nowhere. Any vet would say it was an unhealthy diet but a thorough exam and even blood tests had failed to show any major issues. The judge was unimpressed by photos of healthy looking horses and threw the case out.

One of the horses, a big grey Thoroughbred called Ace, hadn't been out of a pen in fifteen years but there was nothing I could do about it. Finally, a year or so later, that horse had his tail so matted his foot became tangled in it as he stomped away at the hundreds of flies in his little pen. A passerby noticed the poor animal with his foot stuck in the air and called us. Things had gotten worse by then. There was a long-dead opossum in the water trough and the horse's health had declined. We were finally able to seize all the horses.

Around this time, a local vet, Dr. Grant Miller, and some other horse lovers started a group called the Sonoma CHANGE Program, for the sole purpose of assisting animal control with our horse cases. All of the horses received much-needed veterinary and hoof care. They went to loving foster barns and received the best of feed, care and grooming. They were wormed and had their teeth floated, feet trimmed and mats removed. After a long, drawn-out court case, Claudia was given probation and forbidden to own horses for three years. Meanwhile, Ace and the other horses were adopted into loving homes and I saw several of them in their new digs over the following years. As dismal as their lives had been before, they were now filled with affection, days of companionable grazing with other horses, nights in cozy stalls with leafy green alfalfa and a vigorous grooming session most days. Several of them were trained for riding while Ace and an older bay mare were retired to a life of luxury.

It's hard to imagine the sickness of the mind that causes people to feel they must have multiple animals they cannot properly care for. In severe cases the animal are literally dying from lack of care but the owners still believe they are "rescuing" or saving the animals and refuse all assistance. One wealthy elderly woman bought an entire home just for cats. Florence Shaw lived in a wealthy community about forty minutes away and drove her immaculate Mercedes to the cat house each day to care for them. Wait a minute. "Care" is too strong a word. Florence did bring food and occasionally litter, but the urine smell coming from the house was so strong the neighbors complained numerous times. Florence did not respond to numerous notices left on her door and officers had so far been unable to make contact with her. Things came to a head when a neighbor crawled up on a stool and looked in one of the windows. At least twenty-five cats were visible through the window and several dead and sickly cats could be seen as well. This, in combination with the failure of the owner to respond, was enough to finally confiscate the cats.

I was off the day officers were able to force open one of the windows and enter the house, but Jim was working on the case and he told me later how four officers entered the house wearing surgical masks as they confiscated fifty-two terrified, unsocialized cats and kittens. Many of the animals needed veterinary care, a few were already dead, and the filth and ammonia smell was mind-boggling. The house was cluttered with boxes and piles of paper, furniture and endless feces.

Like many hoarders, this woman collected stuff as well as animals, and the place was so packed with junk it was impossible to locate all the cats in the home. She had started with a few rescued cats and then began feeding a few strays. Some of them had litters of kittens and she took in some more unwanted kitties. It all got very out of hand so she bought this house for them and they continued to reproduce. I assisted Jim on some follow-up visits since they had been unable to locate all the cats among the debris in the house. Each day Jim would bait multiple humane traps with canned cat food and the next day would find more cats in the traps.

Another longtime hoarder, Prudence Mayfield, had started out with a couple of little mixed breed dogs and ended up completely overwhelmed. The dogs kept reproducing and neighbors had complained. Every time animal control put the pressure on, Prudence would run an ad in the paper for "Free Chihuahuas" and people would come to the house. She let them take whatever dogs they could catch. Of course, they weren't really Chihuahuas, just small generic short-haired dogs but people took them anyway. Maybe she wasn't quite a true hoarder in the sense that she would part with some of them when we cracked down on her but she was pretty close. The trouble with her method was that over the years when people came to the house they took only the friendliest, cutest dogs they were able to catch. That left the more skittish and homely dogs to reproduce. Already greatly inbred, these dogs developed a strangely uniform look. Most of them had long, pointy, rat-like noses but were horribly overshot, with upper jaws that were much longer than the lower, giving them a gooberish look.

Initially we kept leaving notices but Prudence refused to come to the door or return our calls. She kept her front gate locked and we couldn't even access the property. Things finally came to a head when enough neighbors signed complaints to give us more to go on legally. I left a final notice threatening legal action if she failed to respond and at that point she returned my call. She sounded very upset. When I quickly reassured her I wanted to help, she agreed to meet with us.

My fellow officer, Beth, and I headed out to Prudence's house. When we pulled up, Prudence came out the gate and locked it carefully behind her. She was probably in her fifties, with graying curly hair and an anxious face. We tried to put her at ease as we spoke and advised her we needed to access the property. She initially refused but we finally convinced her she was required by law to show us the animals. She finally gave permission, unlocked the gate and stayed back, sitting dejectedly on the curb.

When we entered the home, I would have bet money no people lived there. The floor was littered with dirt, dried feces and debris. Several small dogs skittered out the open doors and a cat rocketed through a broken window. Sunlight slanted through the opening, illuminating the dust that rose in the air. There was no furniture and the place was nearly bare other than the empty dog food cans that covered every available space. A holey mattress lay on the floor with a tattered blanket and it appeared Prudence slept there. She had gotten back down to only six dogs using her usual method of giving away any dogs that people could catch. There was no sign of abuse and the dogs appeared healthy, but there were several dead dogs on the property. It appeared they had been dead a long time. I asked Prudence about a dead dog on the back porch and she said she had it euthanized at the vet due to old age but hadn't gotten around to burying it yet. I asked how long ago and she said she didn't remember.

Poor Prudence looked teary and in shock and I reminded her we wanted to help her get to a more manageable number of dogs. I told her that to be in compliance with the law all she had to do was give up two of the dogs and allow us to spay and neuter the other four. She seemed relieved. I don't think she ever wanted all those dogs; they just got out of hand. One of the dogs was still a pup of maybe three months. He looked so funny with his pointy nose and overshot bite, but he was young enough to probably come around. Another dog was obviously pregnant and I knew I needed to get her out of there quick before it

110

started all over again. I offered to waive the impound fees if she would sign over the pup and the pregnant dog and she readily agreed. I was able to get a hold of the pup and asked Prudence if she would bring the other dog to me. She looked at me with surprise. "I can't get her. I've never touched her in my life." Oh. The dogs had all been born in this house (the back door was permanently stuck open and the dogs came and went as they pleased) and yet she had never touched them?

Puppies need to be handled daily and experience a variety of new things to learn how to cope and trust people. I netted the little pregnant dog and placed her in a padded carrier. She would go home with me and I would try to get her spayed on Monday when the vet came in. I chatted with Prudence as I worked, hoping to comfort her a bit. She looked traumatized by our intrusion. The strange thing was she herself was clean and well kept, she smelled good, her hair was washed and her legs were even shaved. She worked full-time at a diner in town. No one would have guessed she walked out of this filthy mess every morning. I asked Prudence if she had always lived alone there and she said she had lived there with her mother until her mother died.

Beth and I shot each other an alarmed glance. Could mom be lying around the property somewhere, too? We did one more walk through of the entire place in the guise of searching for more animals but fortunately found no human bodies although I suspiciously eyed a tarp-covered bulge in the yard and gave it a cautious poke with my toe. It proved to just be bags of garbage and I sighed with relief.

Hoarding is a challenging problem. Many hoarders begin collecting animals again immediately after their pets are taken away. We see it all the time. Like the time an attractive woman in her sixties came to our shelter to adopt a dog. She was from another county and seemed perfectly nice, but one of our techs had his suspicions aroused when she wanted to adopt four dogs. On a whim he discreetly called animal control in her county to see what the legal dog limit was there. He also gave them her name to verify there were no prior issues with her. To his surprise, the woman at the other shelter practically came

111

unglued when he gave her the potential adopter's name. She was a notorious hoarder in that county who had just had forty-two dogs and cats removed from her and had been in court over it the previous week. No doubt she would find more animals somewhere, but thanks to a quick-thinking vet tech, our shelter animals didn't add to her count.

20. The Going-Away Cake

"I'm in a gang and I don't want to neuter my dogs."

The speaker of this statement was a burly young man with a shaved head, endless tattoos, a sleeveless white T-shirt and pants so baggy he could have kept a small child in there. We stood in the living room of his house as his equally burly pit bulls sniffed my clothes with interest.

"But if you say I have to, I guess I have to." He looked me in the eye without being challenging or hostile, just telling me how he felt.

I had a lot of respect for this guy. He was up front and wasn't being a jerk. Everyone should be so polite and honest. Of the two main gangs that live in our county, one is noted for being more polite to law enforcement. He apparently belonged to that one. "I'm sorry but it's the law," I said, with a smile. "There are way more dogs than good homes and your dogs were running loose, so I just need to write you a quick fix-it ticket for neuter and licensing and I'll be on my way. May I see your driver's license, please?"

The young man glanced at his watch. "I'm sorry, ma'am, but I was just leaving for jail. I start serving a six-month sentence today and I have to be there in half an hour."

Ok, wow. Now that's one I've never heard before. As I looked around I realized I had arrived in the middle of a going-away party of sorts. Several tough looking, tattooed young men lingered over snacks and cake in the other room while the two dogs, tired of checking me out, wandered around underfoot in search of handouts. When I "recovered," I asked who would be taking responsibility for his dogs while he was away. He glanced into the kitchen at a pleasant-faced, middle-aged woman who was cleaning up. "Hey, Ma!" he called. The woman set down a bowl and grabbed a towel to dry her hands as she walked into the room and greeted me.

The young man said, "Gotta go, Ma." He kissed her cheek and hollered to his friends to hurry up. Several other young men and a girl about ten years old followed him to the door. He did knuckle bumps with his homies, hugged his little sister and headed out, joking with the guys as he went. One of the men gave the girl a high-five. "Great choice of wording on the cake." She laughed with him. "Yeah, I thought it was pretty funny." I was amazed at how everyone, including Mom, seemed totally nonchalant, like her son was running to the store for a gallon of milk instead of a six-month stint in jail. I got back to the business at hand, which was writing Mom a bunch of citations for her son's dogs. We chatted about the dogs as I wrote, but my head was spinning by the time I finished.

On the way out the door I glanced at what was left of the cake. It was your basic grocery store sheet cake, frosted and with wording across the top. I leaned in to read the writing. I mean really, what do you write on a cake for someone who's going to jail? It took me a moment to process what it said and I walked to my truck, climbed in and sat in stunned silence for a moment.

There are certain times in life when you have a real appreciation for how good you have it. I had an intense feeling of gratefulness that my teenaged son was thriving in school, staying out of trouble and not in a gang or headed off to jail. I wasn't being cited for his dogs or saying good-bye to him. But most of all I was glad my daughter wouldn't have had the faintest clue what to put on a

114

going-off-to-jail cake. And she'd never think to write what I'd just seen on that cake. In green frosting across the top it said, "Don't drop the soap."

After work that day I was training Annie in the round pen while the dogs played in the pasture. Spending time with my own animals is very relaxing for me and a great stress reliever. Annie trotted steady circles around me as I stood in the center of the pen, lost in thought. Scott was in the house, working on an essay for class and Nikki, Shay and a friend were hanging out in her room. They had their share of chores and responsibilities, but overall their lives were pretty cushy. I kept thinking of the young man I had dealt with earlier. I hadn't seen any sign of a dad around the house and I wondered about Mom. It seemed like she cared about her kids and yet there was harshness about the whole scene.

Annie was starting to sweat and I called to her to whoa. She stopped immediately and I walked up to her and rubbed her forehead. She leaned into me and I hugged her face gently before I reversed her and asked her to walk so she could cool off. I just couldn't get over how far she had come. I had finally gotten her fairly comfortable with the saddle, but that part had taken a long time. After the incident with James startling her she had twice more jumped out from under it while it was resting on her back. The trick now was to cinch it. I had cinched up a bareback pad on her quite a few times to get her used to the pressure and had spent a lot of time rubbing her all over with ropes and straps, flopping things over her back and pulling them under her belly and legs.

I always liked to give her some exercise before working on something new and now that she was pleasantly relaxed and tired I took her back to the barn and tied her up. I brought the saddle out and stood quietly holding it for a moment, then placed it on her back. So far so good. I scratched her neck and then worked my way around behind her to the other side and lowered the cinch. Coming back to her other side, I scratched her belly and reached carefully under her for the cinch. Drawing it up, I pulled it through, but just then something startled her. She set back hard, fighting the post and leaping around. I tried to stay out of her way while hanging on to the end of the latigo so the saddle wouldn't fall off.

115

She settled down after a moment and I quickly finished cinching her up, just enough to keep it on without freaking her out. I left her tied like that while I mucked out her pen and did a few chores and she finally stood calmly relaxed, one hip cocked. I gave her some grain to increase the pleasant association with the saddle. By now she had a healthy appreciation for grain and she chewed it happily. She jumped a bit when I pulled the saddle off, but it wasn't bad at all, and I led her back toward her pen, still lost in thought. The next thing I knew I was flat on my back, staring at Annie's rapidly retreating hindquarters. She had bolted right over the top of me and knocked me down.

The dogs crowed around me in a concerned circle, trying to lick my face as I surveyed limbs and torso for injuries. I found a couple of tender areas and my jeans were torn at the knee, but I seemed to be okay. Yikes, what had set her off? The flapping of a tarp on a truck headed up the neighbor's driveway seemed a likely culprit. I needed to remember she was born a wild horse and not to be distracted when working with her.

Annie usually calmed down quickly after her panics and she was grazing happily by the time I pulled myself up and walked over to her. She followed me back to the barn like an old plow horse as I returned her to her pen and fed her and Joe and Roanie. Later that night, surveying my bruises in the bathtub, I thought, she's making wonderful progress but she has a long way to go.

21. Cockfighting Raid

The emergency room physician, Dr. Peter Ellers, was a warm and welcoming animal lover and he chatted eagerly with me as he stitched up my lacerated arm. I hadn't even had to wait for hours like I had on some previous ER visits. I was his first animal control officer with injuries resulting from a cockfighting raid and this was new territory for him.

The doctor quizzed me at length about cockfighting and about my job in general. When he had inserted the final suture he tossed the needle onto the tray, broke out his iPhone and showed me dozens of photos of his three beautiful dogs, two Golden Retrievers and a pit bull. This guy had a gorgeous wife and two teenage kids at home; I caught a glimpse of them as he flipped through his photos. But by far the most photos were of the dogs. He adored his family but when he walked in the door after a long day of sewing up the local Dogcatcher, it was his dogs who greeted him like he was the returning messiah. His kids might look up from their texting and offer a monosyllabic response to his hellos. His wife would be better, with a quick peck on the cheek and a "How was your day?" but the dogs couldn't get enough of him. Their joy on his arrival was unlike any he received anywhere else in his life. To them he was better than a walking, talking rump roast. I walked out of the ER, still grinning at the doctor's enthusiasm for his canine buddies and headed back to work. I had a huge cockfighting report to write.

The call had come in innocently enough; we get lots of cockfighting calls that don't really turn out to be much. Don't get me wrong, they are usually legitimate from a standpoint of people engaging in illegal cockfighting. The problem lies in catching them at it and proving it. Of course, there is no other reason anyone would have 200 roosters in individual cages with their spurs, combs and wattles removed. But it's not against the law to have 200 roosters. In order to prosecute we have to catch people in the act of fighting them or at least with the slashers or other illegal paraphernalia. Cockfighters know this, and those things are always kept locked up and out of sight.

I had been given a call of a cockfight in progress at an address on Walker Road, but was to meet up with a sheriff's deputy at the corner of Walker and Patterson before advancing. My coworker, Jim, had overheard the call and was close by so he pulled up about the same time I did. Tall and solidly built, Jim is an experienced officer and a good guy to have around in a pinch.

We got out and walked up to where the deputy was waiting. Carmen Alexander, the sheriff's deputy, was an attractive brunette with a big smile and a firm handshake. I looked at her neatly uniformed, petite frame and wondered how well she would hold up against the bad guys. Her gun seemed bigger than she was. Carmen advised us dispatch was getting more information and this was probably a major fight. We were to wait for more backup.

We leaned against the patrol car and shielded our eyes from the sun as we looked in the direction of the address we had been given. The place was surrounded by a solid board fence about six feet high and all that was visible on the property from our viewpoint was a long, enclosed equipment shed.

In the distance I heard the *chop chop chop* of a helicopter. Jim looked up. "That's Henry One." Henry One is our local sheriff's helicopter. I wondered where it was headed. My answer came quickly. It was headed our way and was

118

soon circling the property we were observing. Almost at once swarms of men began fleeing the property, running in every direction, jumping fences and racing through nearby fields. Cars began to peel out of the driveway. Carmen jumped in her patrol car and gunned it forward, neatly cutting off the dead-end street. She then jumped out and stood ready with her hand on her gun. Tiny as she was, she made an imposing picture. The drivers, seeing their way blocked, abandoned their vehicles and headed for the fields, except for one elderly gentleman who optimistically continued toward us. He stopped his battered green pickup truck in front of us and smiled reassuringly. Carmen reached into the truck through the open window, grabbed his keys from the ignition and tossed them into the back. "Get out of the vehicle and put your hands on your head," she demanded. He began to explain that he had just taken a wrong turn and was on his way out. He claimed he didn't have a clue what all the fuss was about. Yeah, right! Carmen had him neatly cuffed and in her patrol car before he knew what happened. We could see the crisscross pattern of scars on his hands as she put the cuffs on him, likely the result of years of handling fighting roosters. She glanced at me and Jim and nodded toward the truck while she questioned him. We went to the vehicle and began to search for cockfighting evidence but there was none to be found, probably all left at the fight. Still, it's illegal to even attend a cockfight. He was busted either way.

In the meantime, there wasn't much Jim or I could do but sit back and watch the chaos. We were waiting for backup and listening to our hip radios, as the helicopter continued to circle, radioing locations to officers on the ground. Several horses in a nearby pasture galloped around frantically, spooked by the helicopter and the people running everywhere. More animal control officers, sheriff's deputies and police officers from every town in the area were en route. The problem was every time an officer got near our location they had to stop to arrest fleeing suspects. Two of our animal control officers were flagged down by a highly agitated teenage boy who had fled his home after two suspects burst in his back door trying to hide. Our officers went inside and handcuffed the men and detained them until deputies arrived.

The sheriff's office was flooded with trespassing calls. "Yes, hello, police? There are two men carrying chickens through my backyard and now they are hiding in my bushes!" Or "Hi, yeah, um, my Rottweiler has a guy cornered on top of my tool shed."

When a couple of deputies finally arrived to escort us onto the scene, we entered the property. Every single person had fled except for the poor guy in the full leg cast and crutches. It sucks when your best buddies leave you and your crutches behind when the cockfight gets raided. He sat gloomily in his car as officers confiscated wads of money from his wallet and placed him under arrest.

From inside the enclosed shed we'd seen from the street came the deafening din of what sounded like hundreds of roosters crowing from their carrying cages. We entered the shed. What a sight it was. The shed was divided into three large rooms. Piles of dead, bloody roosters were tossed carelessly in corners. We walked through each room documenting and photographing everything. There were two fighting pits, each with a pair of dying roosters in it. The birds had probably continued their bloody battles unabated long after their handlers had fled the coop. All were near death, and Jim humanely dispatched them. He glanced at me afterwards and in his eyes I read a strong distaste for the necessary procedure. I didn't blame him. I didn't like it either and if he hadn't done it I would have had to. "Thanks buddy," I said simply.

Everywhere we looked we saw boxes of razor-sharp slashers, some in fancy, beautifully designed cases with velvet lining. Roosters fight by striking their opponent repeatedly with their legs and have naturally occurring claw-like spurs on their legs. Slashers are evil-looking blades, a type of miniature knife that is fitted to the roosters spurs before the fight. We recorded and photographed the waxed string and scissors used to attach the lethal blades.

Continuing on, we saw the orange slices the handlers let the roosters peck at before the fight to give them energy and the scales for weighing them. We saw betting slips for keeping track of wagers. In one room was a long buffet-style table lined with rows of delicious looking Mexican dishes of every kind. The smell was wonderful, but the entire scene made me sick to my stomach and I turned away.

Outside the shed and seated in a large group in front of it were a number of handcuffed suspects who had been returned to the property. We had to walk past them as we worked, and I took a look at them out of the corner of my eye. Cockfighting is a strongly cultural pastime. All of them appeared to be Hispanic, most were young and all were male. Their money had been confiscated, they were under arrest and many of them would most likely be deported. I wondered if it would deter them from this barbaric activity in the future.

Other officers began to arrive and assist us and I began the job of loading up the birds in our trucks. Most of the live roosters were in small wooden carrying boxes but a few were in the larger warm-up pens where they had been placed in preparation for the next fight. I had to reach in, grab them and place them in empty carriers. One of the roosters had obviously already fought; some of its feathers hung down with drying blood on them. He must have been the winner because he was still alive and vigorous. I glanced quickly at the legs to check for slashers and, seeing none, reached in and made a grab for him. Unfortunately, the bloody feathers had hidden the slasher on a leg.

Most fighting roosters are not human-aggressive but this bird was in a highly agitated state and he instantly attacked me with ferocious determination. I was stunned by the power of the blows, like a stab from a knife in the hand of strong man. The blade went deep into the inside of my left forearm and wrist several times before I could get a hold of him and place him in a cage. I grabbed the pen from my shirt pocket and wrote SLASHER ATTACHED in big letters across the top of the wooden cage so the shelter technicians wouldn't be injured taking this him out of the carrier. One casualty was enough. I glanced at my arm and was shocked to see gaping wounds and blood flowing down onto my hand. Jim walked in then, and his eyes bugged. "What happened?!"

"One still had a slasher on," I said.

He grabbed a nearby roll of paper towels and pressed it to my arm but the room began to spin and I felt like I was going to black out. I looked around for somewhere to lie down and staggered toward a sheet on the ground that had been used to cover the cages. I lay down on my side, hoping to avoid fainting, but began to lose consciousness. Jim radioed dispatch requesting an ambulance and was turned away from me. (He would never admit it, but he looked a little faint, too.) I called out weakly, "I don't need an ambulance." I didn't want to make a fuss and I was embarrassed about not being more careful. Plus, I've always suffered from low blood pressure and am prone to fainting. I could feel my other hand, the one holding the paper towels, begin to slip off the wound and I wasn't sure how bad I was bleeding. I felt so weak I couldn't seem to hold pressure on the wound and I was worried about blood loss. I fought to stay alert but the darkness closed in and I could only hear, as if a long distance away, the fading sounds of Jim on the radio and the roosters crowing.

After a moment consciousness returned and I was feeling more alert but I lay still on my side on the floor. A deputy walked in and saw me lying on the floor with my bloody paper towels and went as white as a sheet. He pointed a shaking finger at me. "Uh, uh, uh….!" Jim looked up, saw the officer's face and said, "An ambulance is on the way." I spoke again, a little more loudly this time, "I don't need an ambulance."

"Too late," said Jim, firmly. "They're on their way."

I attempted to sit. "Well, call them back and cancel, I'll be fine," I said. I knew I needed stitches but certainly not an ambulance. I was annoyed as it was to have to leave my call in the middle of everything. Just then, two strapping young paramedics entered the shed. The bleeding had slowed by now and they cleaned and covered the wounds and wrapped my arm in layers of gauze. I declined a ride in the ambulance and a fellow officer, Beth Cappelli, offered to drive me to the hospital. An attractive and hard-working redhead, Beth is easy-going and fun. It was a relief to have her there in a stressful situation.

As we walked out to Beth's truck we passed the group of men under arrest. By then at least fifty men in handcuffs sat in the driveway. A deputy was counting the confiscated betting money and I overheard him say, "I'm up to

$34,000." I felt like I'd been gone a long time, things had changed so much since I'd arrived just an hour ago. A big prison bus parked out front waited to take the men to jail and the entire dead-end street was lined with animal control trucks and patrol cars from every law enforcement agency for miles around. There was the ambulance, along with a fire truck and the local news crew. As we passed I heard the news photographer say to his companion, "Did she have her arm bandaged before?" I ducked quickly behind the fire truck and made a beeline for Beth's truck. The last thing I wanted was to have my injury blasted all over the evening news. I was mortified enough to be hurt on the job without that.

Thankfully, my gashes healed quickly with just some ugly scars to show for my carelessness. It could have been much worse, as one of the scars ran right alongside one of the major veins in my wrist. Scott was horrified at the time but later said, "Wow, Mom, that's so cool. You're the only mom I know with cockfighting raid scars!" It's good to know my kid can brag about his mom to his friends. It's the age-old game: my mom is more bad-ass than your mom! I didn't show Paul the wounds for a few days and downplayed them as much as possible. He knew what had happened, of course, but he worries about my job enough as it is without seeing the grisly evidence of what can happen.

Other similar cockfighting calls I've had were on a smaller scale and involved less blood loss on my part. In one case the arrested men were handcuffed near the pit as I gathered up the birds. Two injured birds lay on their backs in the pit. As I approached them, in passable English, one of the men said, "Be careful, ma'am. They still have their slashers on." These guys had been arrested, all their money was confiscated, and were losing the roosters they had paid big money for not to mention spent all of their free time training and conditioning. I looked at them with surprise. I would have thought they would have loved to see Little Miss Animal Control slashed to bloody bits, but they looked genuinely concerned about me. (I could have used them at the other raid!) As much as I hate cockfighting, these men were not monsters, they were young and uneducated and came from a culture where cockfighting is a very big

123

deal.

As I reached carefully for the birds and turned them over to place them into a carrier they revived almost instantly and were ready to go at it again. One of the detained men called out to me, "Which one is stronger?"

"Well, I guess the red one," I replied, without thinking.

There was a whoop of triumph from one of the men. "I told you red was gonna win," he bragged to his buddy.

I felt a flash of anger. "But now this beautiful bird is dying for your entertainment!"

The room fell silent as I continued to load up roosters and equipment.

In another case we were called to a home where someone reported a cockfight. There must have been just a few people practicing with the birds because all was quiet when we arrived with two animal control officers and a deputy. The owners were Spanish-speaking, but I managed to get the point across I needed to see the roosters and we all walked out to the barn. About a hundred roosters, with combs, spurs and wattles removed, sat in individual cages, classic fighting birds. There was a locked shed, but the resident had a very truthful-sounding story about how the birds and shed belonged to his cousin Jesse in Mexico and no, he did not know his last name and no, he did not have a key.

There was a darling little boy of about five years old on the property. His name was Jose, and I smiled and tried to talk to him to set him at ease. I love kids and didn't want him to be afraid of law enforcement. I told him the birds were pretty and asked him how old he was, but he looked at me solemnly with his big brown eyes and didn't say a word. Thinking he didn't speak English I tried a few words of Spanish and got the same result. He followed me and Officer Tom Ross around as we looked for something we could use to prove illegal activity, but we found nothing. Tom found a life-sized stuffed rooster with numerous peck holes in it and I photographed it. At that, our little companion's face lit up. He pointed at the stuffed bird and with a voice of authority, said, "Dat's to teach da woosters to fight!" He was so cute and so proud of his knowledge that Tom and I had to stifle a laugh. His mama roared around the corner of the barn about then, yelling at him in Spanish to get in the house, and that was the last we saw of little Jose. I hope he wasn't in too much trouble.

22. Easy Money

A few days after my cockfighting injury, I had an appointment to assist an acquaintance with some livestock. A friend of a friend, Helen Gilly, was in her sixties and had recently had surgery. She offered to pay anyone $100 who would come and trim the feet of her two llamas and a goat. Helen had rescued the group years before and they enjoyed the run of her beautiful tree-lined pasture. Recently she had noticed the hooves were getting long and decided she had better address the issue but was unable to do it herself. I needed the money and showed up on my day off.

So much for easy money. The llamas hadn't been touched in eight years, two miniature donkeys also needed foot trims, and the animals were loose in a ten-acre field. After what seemed like forever, we succeeded in coaxing the llamas with grain to a smaller corral. They stared at us suspiciously and took agonizingly slow, cautious steps before finally reaching the gate. There, they stretched out their long necks and looked toward the grain while contemplating the universe. I was starting to wonder if I should pitch a tent and wait it out or just tear my hair out in frustration. After about a year, they finally entered the pen and I slammed the gate shut behind them.

My experience with llamas is limited. I think they're adorable but I'm leery of their perpetually offended expressions and penchant for spitting foul-smelling stomach contents on anyone who annoys them. I suspected that wrestling them around to do their feet might be considered annoying, but, to my surprise, I was able to get a rope on them with no disgusting repercussions.

Once I had a halter on the first llama, I tied him to the fence and began to attempt a pedicure. The 300-pound llama jumped, kicked and repeatedly yanked his foot away from me, but I doggedly persisted, knowing full well it probably wasn't the best time to be doing this. I could feel the sutures of my lacerated arm pulling each time he struggled. Still, I couldn't quit now. I trimmed one foot and then he sullenly quit fighting and lay down, completely covering all of his feet with his big wooly body. He stared passively into the distance while I struggled to pull one foot at a time into reach. I was dripping with sweat by the time I trimmed all four. The second llama added his own variations to the rodeo.

But the time I finished the two llamas, my injured arm ached badly, and I still had the goat and two donkeys to do. I was beginning to wonder if this was worth the hundred dollars, but to my delight the goat seemed quite tame and gentle, though he did occasionally attempt to use his long, curved horns to scratch his back and poked me in the rear instead.

The donkeys were adorable with shaggy coats and long fringed bangs that hung appealingly over big brown eyes. They stood only about as tall as the goat, which turned out to be more of an issue than I could have expected. When working with horse's feet you can grip the hoof between your knees and have both hands free to work. Because donkeys are too small for that, I tried to tuck their tiny feet between my ankles and grip them that way. Not easy to do, but I was making some progress on the first donkey when her companion began sniffing her back end and then decided to take advantage of her compromised position. Before I could react, he optimistically threw himself on top of her and began to pound away. Being decidedly not in the mood, she launched some rapid-fire kicks in his direction. The first blows glanced off my arm, partially ripping the bandage before I could stumble out of the way. The lead tore loose from my grasp and she bolted up the hill with the male in hot pursuit. I was bruised and winded by the time I captured both of the offenders and tied them to separate posts.

Ignoring the blood seeping through the bandage on my arm as best I could, I finished the female and started on the male. He seemed slightly subdued but kept giving her the eye and calling endearments to her as I worked. At last I finished, feeling beaten in body and spirit. Helen, seeing what an ordeal it had been, gave me an extra $25.

Later, in the bathtub, Paul helped me remove the battered bandage and we dismally surveyed the formerly immaculate row of sutures. He shook his head and turned away briefly before helping me rewrap the arm. I had been so impressed by Dr. Ellers' suturing job and was thinking it would hardly leave a scar. I had no such fantasy now. The flesh had pulled apart somewhat and each suture had pulled through the skin enough to cause a small cut on each one. To this day the scars are quite apparent on my forearm.

23. Tracking Down the Bad Guys

The photographs in an email message on my computer showed a nice-looking sorrel stallion with fairly standard markings of blaze and two rear socks and a bay stallion with a snippet of white on the muzzle. The horses had originally been seized in a neglect case up north in Amador County and removed from the owner along with five other horses. The photos had been taken after a period of rehabilitation at that county's animal control facility, so the animals looked pretty good by then. Unfortunately, however, there had been some mishandling of the case and the animals had been ordered to be returned to the neglectful owner. It is one of the frustrating parts of the job: an obviously undeserving person can be given another chance to mistreat their animals. Fortunately, before the owner picked up, animal control staff microchipped the horses as a means of permanent identification. (Microchips are about the size of a grain of rice and can be implanted under an animal's skin.)

I continued to read the email. Soon after the horses were returned to the owner, the owner violated the conditions of his agreement and the agency was again given permission to seize the animals. This time, only five horses were

129

present. The owner claimed he had sold the other two and couldn't remember the buyer's names or any other information. After receiving a tip that the owner had relatives in our county, we were contacted to look into the matter.

I looked closely at the suspect address. It looked familiar. In seconds I verified the address on Pine Bluff Road was the property where I had a felony horse case pending.

The previous summer an emaciated bay gelding had been reported in a field of cows. When several women with a local horse rescue group drove by and saw the pathetic creature they stopped to confront the resident. The man said that he owned the cattle but had no idea who the horse belonged to and claimed it had just appeared. He gave the women permission to remove the animal. They took it home and contacted us. I responded, photographed the horse and gave permission for immediate veterinary care. Sadly, the horse was in such bad shape it couldn't be saved.

Suspecting the cattle owner was attempting to avoid prosecution, I met with him to begin an investigation for cruelty and neglect. The man sounded utterly sincere when he claimed never to have seen the horse before. I contacted all the neighbors, who corroborated the story. They had noticed the horse for the first time on the morning of the day it was found. I, too, had never noticed the horse among the cows the many times I had driven past this field.

The horse, it seemed, had been abandoned there, probably at night since no one had seen it. The next task was to find out who was responsible. I began to question neighbors farther away and to research some of our prior horse calls in the area.

The case received quite a bit of press. I got a call from a local investigator for the District Attorney's office offering to help. Tim Dempsey was a horse person as well as an investigator and was interested in assisting me with the case if I didn't mind. Of course I didn't mind. I could use all the help I could get, and Tim had a lot of experience investigating cases.

What a stroke of luck. Tim and I met up and began a systematic investigation, brainstorming and going door to door. We doubted the abandoned horse had been hauled there by trailer as there wasn't an area to pull over, unless they had parked down the street and led the animal to the field. We looked into a skinny horse of the same color that Tim had noticed a few weeks earlier in a field beside a house a few miles away. Our agency had already investigated that horse and found it to be thin due to advanced old age but receiving good feed and veterinary care. Still, it did match the description. Maybe they got tired of caring for it and dumped it in a stranger's field. Who knows why people do what they do. Tim and I drove to that house, but when we pulled up, there she was, grazing in her field. Another dead end.

A donation fund was started by the rescue group to provide a reward for clues in the case and flyers with photos were distributed in the area. Tips began to trickle in but nothing fruitful came for several weeks. Finally, I spoke to a caller who thought she knew where the horse had come from. She gave the address on Pine Bluff Road and stated that she had bought a horse from that address and had considered buying another horse with the same markings as the gelding in the reward photos. She remembered the markings because they were the same as her other horse. The horse had been in good shape when she saw it only six months before. The next day another caller offered up the same address.

Looking up the address I saw that I had been out there for a loose steer the year before and I recalled the horses I could see in the pens had looked healthy. With Beth's help, I had caught the steer and returned it to someone on the property and had no reason to investigate further. Another complaint had come in sometime longer ago regarding training methods that appeared too harsh, but the officer who had investigated found paddocks of horses with no sign of abuse. The address was less than a mile from the field where the horse was dumped but just beyond the area where Tim and I had gone door to door.

Tim and I met up and began to question neighbors surrounding the suspect address. No one at the first two houses knew anything, but a woman at the house adjacent to the address was a gold mine of information.

Yes, there had been a bay horse next door that had looked good and then gone downhill rapidly and become very thin. She hadn't seen it for several weeks now. Tim glanced at me with a raised eyebrow. The horse had been found abandoned three weeks earlier. "You don't have any photos that might include that horse in it, do you?" Tim asked her. "Maybe as background when you were taking pictures on your property?"

I looked at Tim with surprise. Why would she have pictures of her neighbor's horses? But the woman jumped up and went in the other room. "Hang on," she called out. "I have videos of the horses."

Tim grinned at me as I stared at him in shock. I guess that's why he's the investigator.

The woman handed Tim a CD and we took down her information and thanked her profusely. She had been the complainant on the harsh training methods and had videotaped her neighbor's horses when they were tied up for several hours on some days. She had shown the tape to the animal control officer who investigated, but no violation of the law was visible, so he hadn't mentioned the videotape in his investigation.

Back at Tim's office we watched the grainy video with renewed hope. We saw some horses tied to a tree on the suspect property. They looked healthy and none matched the description of the abandoned horse. We continued watching as the video started and then stopped, apparently filmed over some length of time. Finally, Tim saw something. He pointed to a horse barely visible in the background behind another horse. "Stop it right there," he said. I pushed the pause button and we leaned in to get a better look. It was a bay horse with a star on its forehead just like the abandoned horse. That's a common color and marking and it was hard to see clearly, but it was still a possibility.

I grabbed my photos of the abandoned horse and studied them. The horse in the video had been in good condition, not emaciated like the abandoned horse. The face certainly could have been the same. The abandoned horse had one right hind sock, but we couldn't see the legs well in the video. The long grass hid them. We spent some time advancing and reversing the tape, hoping to get a better view of the legs. "I have a friend who can enlarge this at the crime lab," said Tim. "Maybe we can see better." I was thrilled. Animal control

132

doesn't have much access to stuff like that. I thanked him and headed back to work.

Several more weeks of careful investigation followed, and we finally determined the horse in the video was most likely the same horse seen abandoned in the field. Tim interviewed the original informants again and ferreted out some more clues, including a possible name of the horse's former owner. Online, I found the property owner's name and printed his photo from the DMV. The name of the horse owner was different from the property owner. Further complicating things, we learned that multiple people boarded horses at the property. Still, a property owner could share responsibility for allowing a horse to get in that condition.

We finally had several suspects and their photos and I was eager to move in and make some arrests. I was haunted by the suffering the horse had gone through. Tim, however, seemed to be stalling. Sure, he had extensive knowledge of the law and endless experience in prosecuting cases, but we weren't ready? What did he know? I chomped at the bit while he continued to patiently work away at the case, making absolutely sure we had uncovered every possible bit of evidence.

And more information came. We learned that one of the possible suspects was on probation for domestic violence. The other had a drug history, and there was a protective German shepherd on the property.

It was finally time to move in. At first I imagined stopping by some afternoon to nab the bad guy with Tim and a sheriff's deputy, but Tim had bigger plans. Tim and I arranged to meet at a corner market down the street from the address at 5:00 a.m. on a Wednesday morning. Dr. Grant Miller, our horse vet and a founder of the Sonoma CHANGE Program, would be there. He also had extensive experience in cruelty and neglect cases. My supervisor, Bob, would come along with law enforcement backup. This was going to be a surprise raid.

When I pulled up to the market parking lot in the dark that morning I was shocked by what awaited me. There were about twenty cops, along with Dr

Miller, Tim and Bob. The officers were chatting quietly among themselves and carefully checking their multiple firearms. They greeted me politely and went back to discussing the plan of attack.

They would head in first and secure the scene. I was somewhat disappointed to not be included in the initial raid, but I had to admit that it made sense. I have neither sidearm's nor training in that sort of thing. "What about the dog?" I asked.

"Show me how to use the catch pole?" said Tim. "I'll take care of the dog." I gave him the crash course in catch pole use and they headed off while Dr. Miller, Bob and I waited in the parking lot, listening nervously to our radios to hear what was happening.

It was all over in a matter of minutes. The dog took one look at the approaching army and fled to the back of the property. The scene was secured, the residents detained and we were cleared to enter.

As we arrived on the property I could see the wisdom of Tim's timing. We arrived under cover of darkness and while people were still asleep, but the first rays of sunshine were beginning to lighten the eastern sky, making our investigation infinitely easier. Tim was busy questioning the suspects while the cops searched the house. Several weapons had already been found, a violation of probation.

Bob, Dr. Miller and I began our investigation, examinations and documentation of the eighteen horses on the property. All appeared healthy as we worked our way from horse to horse, photographing and mapping their locations. Besides some feces buildup in some of the paddocks, they looked fine in the early morning light flooding the scene.

Then we entered the barn. The first stall was boarded shut with only a narrow opening at the top of a half door about six inches deep. Probably a storage or feed area, I thought, and then I heard heavy footsteps inside. I tried to peer through the gap but it was pitch black in there. I found my flashlight on my belt and shined it inside. Spotlighted was a large Andalusia stallion.

Spooked by the glare of the flashlight, he startled as I took in the scene.

Feces were built up against the floor and walls, nearly a foot deep in spots. The floor was uneven and pools of urine rested in the low areas. A tub of dirty water stood in one corner near a residue of hay where the poor animal had been forced to eat off the filthy floor. There wasn't a single window or any type of ventilation, and the only opening was the gap above the door. The reek of ammonia coming through that gap was so bad I was forced to back away and take a gulp of fresh air.

Shining my light back on the stallion, I could see he appeared healthy despite his dark and dismal conditions. I hollered to Dr. Miller, who was wrapping up an exam of a yearling in one of the paddocks. Dr. Miller is a handsome and dedicated vet who usually spends half his time on horse ranches fighting off the advances of female horse owners. He is an outstanding horse doctor and the picture of professionalism, but he is passionate about horses and I knew he wasn't going to like this. He grabbed my flashlight and shone the beam into the dark. He was furious at the sight of the stallion in dark, filthy stall. "Damn them!" he yelled. He began ripping at the board above the half door with his hands, yanking at the boards. "I'd like to get my hands on whoever did this!" I felt the same way but stayed quiet. I grabbed a hoof rasp from a nearby shelf and handed it to him.

The horse snorted and bolted around the tiny stall as Dr. Miller continued his assault on the door. The top was nailed shut with plywood, and the bottom half of the door was secured with a heavy bolt through a hole drilled in the door and frame. The big nut on the end was rusted to the bolt. Dr. Miller smashed it furiously with the rasp. His anger lent power to his attack on the door and at last I heard the plywood splinter as he ripped it free. I'm sure we both thought the same thing. How long had this animal been kept in this tiny dark dungeon to let it rust shut like that?

Dr. Miller eased the door open and grabbed a halter and lead off the hook on the wall. His entire demeanor changed as he slowly entered the stall. Stallions can be unpredictable and sometimes dangerous, especially when they haven't been out of a stall in months or, in this case, even years.

Speaking softly, Dr. Miller approached the stallion. "Hey buddy, what's going on with you? You're going to be okay, buddy." He placed a hand on the heavily muscled neck and began to slowly massage the neck and withers. The stallion's skin twitched and the ears flickered back and forth, but he allowed Dr. Miller to slip a halter on him. I opened the door and Dr. Miller led the stallion into the sunshine.

Despite his hideous home and some manure stains on his coat, the stallion was a magnificent animal. A dappled gray of about 1,200 pounds, he had the gorgeous arched neck and graceful lines of his breed. The unbrushed mane and tail, though tousled, were naturally wavy and added to the picture.

He looked around for a moment, head held high, as if unable to believe the sight of sunlight, green grass, and other horses, and as he did, we gazed at him, mesmerized by his beauty. Then he exploded suddenly into the air. Like a lippazan stallion performing his signature move, he leapt straight up, front legs folded under him, rear legs kicked straight out behind him. His kick narrowly missed Dr. Miller's vet truck, which was parked beside the barn. It seemed he would go up forever, a Pegasus released from his prison. Both startled and awed by his unexpected launch, I stumbled out of his way and nearly fell on my butt.

Dr. Miller neatly reined the stallion into a circle, but the horse grew more agitated. Working quickly, we moved him into a stall with a window. His halter removed, with ears pinned back, the stallion immediately leaned through the window and tried to bite me. Stallions often live a life of solitude and frustration and can be hostile or desperate in their attempts to escape. That probably explained why he was kept boarded up. But at the very least he should have had access to a spacious, safely fenced outdoor area. With an experienced trainer and some exercise and enrichment he could be a very different animal. We gave the stallion some hay and filled a water tub for him and went on to document the scene. There were several more stallions in the barn, none quite as bad as the first, but it was no way to live.

At one point I passed Tim, who had one of the suspects in his patrol car and was questioning him. I overheard the man tell Tim he had sold the horse to the other suspect who still kept it on the first man's property and lived there as well. When the horse started losing weight he told the owner the horse needed veterinary care. The other man, when interviewed, stated that two of his horses had escaped together. One had gone north, the other had gone south. (That right there was suspicious; horses are herd animals and will usually try to stay together.) He said he had caught and brought the first horse home. The second he claimed he couldn't catch so he just ran it into the field where it was found and shut the gate. The abandoned horse had been so weak and decrepit that it was ridiculous to think the owner couldn't capture him. Most likely, the horse had been dumped there because the owner was irresponsible and didn't want to pay to care for him.

In the end, both men were arrested and then released on bail to await trial. I had served written warnings that the stalls were to be cleaned daily, and ventilation provided. When I returned the next day to check on the horses I was pleased to see that about ten men were hard at work shoveling out the filthy stalls and two windows had been cut in the Andalusia's stall. Our department was given permission to come by anytime and check on the horses. I stopped by unannounced at least once a week while awaiting trial, so when the call came in to search for the missing stallions from Amador County it was easy to check on.

I studied the markings on the photos of the missing horses and slipped a microchip scanner in my pocket as I pulled up at the barn. By then, the multiple owners of horses on the property were used to my stopping in and usually greeted me pleasantly. A young man named Mario came along with me as I wandered the property looking for the Amador horses. I hadn't told him about the missing horses, so he would have assumed I was just on my regular visit.

I found a sorrel stallion whose markings matched and my heart pounded hopefully as I slipped into his pen to scan for a microchip. Mario was outside the pen and behind me as I slipped the scanner out of my pocket and passed it over the neck of the horse in front of me. Within seconds the cheerful beep-beep sounded, signaling that a chip had been found. To my amazement,

Mario asked, "Does he have a chip?" Now what the heck does a twenty-year-old Mexican ranch hand know about microchips? And I thought I had been so sly.

Now I was worried. If he suspected that I knew about the horse he might try to remove him and hide him before Amador Animal Control could pick him up. I tried to be casual. "Oh, lots of horses have them now," I said, and I moved on to the next horse, making small talk with Mario as we went. The bay stallion was not on the property.

The minute I pulled out of the driveway I was on the phone to Amador County. They would pick up the stallion the next day. I could only hope he would still be there.

The following day I waited for the Amador animal control officers in a parking lot down the street. As soon as they pulled up we conferred for a moment and then they followed me down the street and into the driveway on Pine Bluff Drive. For the first time since I had started going there, no one was around. Usually groups of men were caring for their various horses and hanging around the barn. I haltered up the stallion as quickly as possible and led him to the open stock trailer. He hesitated for only a moment before leaping inside. An impound notice was placed on his pen and we were out of the driveway in less than five minutes. It had gone as smoothly as it could have gone.

Meanwhile, the original case that Tim and I had worked on so hard dragged on for some time with endless witnesses and excellent testimony from Dr. Miller regarding the terrible condition and suffering the abandoned horse had endured. Dr. Miller also passionately described the filth and ammonia stench of the closed stall where the stallion had been kept. Many horse lovers from the community attended the trial and waited tensely as it wrapped up. The final verdict — guilty — was met with high fives and sighs of relief from everyone involved. The bay horse had received justice. The defendants were sentenced to jail time and forbidden to own horses again.

24. How to Get Bit By a Dog

Two minor puncture wounds were just visible above Robert Wall's ankle. The old man held up his slacks, revealing part of his skinny white leg as he told me how the dog had rushed off its property and bitten him while he was on his morning walk. As I took the report he began to tell me about all the other bites he had received. He even took a little notebook out of his pocket and flipped through it as he detailed each one.

Mr. Wall was quiet and soft spoken. A widower and a talented oil painter, he spent every morning walking miles around his suburban neighborhood. He lived in an upscale area without a lot of loose dogs and I was puzzled by his being bitten so many times. I make a living dealing with aggressive dogs every day and am rarely bitten. I wondered what it was about him that incited normally docile canines to violence. I mean, it's not like the old guy wrapped his legs in bacon before he set out each morning.

I asked him to tell me about each bite, how it happened and what his reactions were to the dogs. He told me that when he saw a dog he would yell in an attempt to frighten it away. As it approached he would begin to flail around, kicking and swinging his arms and continuing to yell. Wow…. That's probably more effective than bacon. Jump around like a wounded antelope and hope the predator doesn't eat you.

Mr. Wall hadn't reported most of the bites but this was the second time I had responded to a bite report from him. In both cases the dogs appeared to be mild mannered, well-cared-for dogs that rarely left their property. In this current case the dog was a ten-year-old Lab mix that had never bitten a soul in his life. Of course, no one deserves to be bitten while out minding his own business, but I could see how Mr. Wall's behavior could be a contributing factor in these situations.

In another dog bite case a toddler had been bitten after climbing onto the back of a relative's elderly, arthritic Cattle Dog. Not only that, but the dog had bitten before. The child's father explained all this to me in loud, angry tones while demanding that I euthanize the dog immediately. Apparently the family had been visiting the wife's sister and the child had wandered into the other room where the dog was lying on his bed and chewing a bone. The child sustained a minor puncture to the hand. I had to wonder what the parents were thinking, letting their baby roam around someone else's home unattended where there was a dog with a history of biting.

One man walked out of the bank and was probably distracted pondering his financial situation when he hopped into a blue Honda Accord. Unfortunately, it wasn't his blue Honda Accord. The big black mixed breed in the vehicle took offense to his intrusion and the man received a hearty chomp to the arm for his inattention.

We do see some very serious bites in this line of work, but most are minor. Sometimes things sound much worse than they really are. A panicked 911 report of a Great Dane attacking a child at a bus stop and dragging him across the road had me horrified until I got the full story. "Monty," a ten-month-old fawn Dane weighing around 130 pounds had escaped his yard and bounded down to the bus stop in delight to play with some kids. Monty bounced around like a circus elephant for a few minutes while the kids petted him and laughed at his antics.

All might have been well had Monty not spied the fuzzy Elmo backpack attached to young Johnny. Grabbing Elmo he shook him back and forth a few times and then decided he needed to take his prize home and headed back toward his driveway. Unfortunately, Elmo was still attached to Johnny. Johnny wasn't even particularly upset; he just wanted his backpack, but to the witness who saw the event from her window at a distance it looked like total carnage. The only casualty was Elmo, who was promptly replaced by Monty's apologetic owners.

25. Oh, Deer

   , The old man stood clutching his walker on his front porch. He was so small and frail he looked as if he might blow away. The lined face lit up with a smile and his thin shock of white hair fluttered in the breeze as he greeted me, but the smile faded to concern as he looked me up and down. "Sweetheart, you're going to need some help," he said.

   "Let's see what we've got first and I'll call for backup if I need it." I said, looking around. "Where is the deer, Mr. Lockwood?"

   He pointed to the end of the deck. "He's good and stuck," he said. "I thought they would send a big strong man."

   The gentleman was in no way being unpleasant. He was truly worried about my welfare. While he was talking I had walked down to the end of the deck where a young spike-horned buck hung from the deck rails by his hips. He had tried to squeeze through, but the hips are the widest point on most animals (I think they're the widest point on me, too!) and now he hung forlornly with his front feet dangling a foot or so from the ground.

   In the past some officers had sawed through railings in a case like this

142

or used a jack to pry metal bars apart, but I had discovered an easy solution almost by accident after a friend's dog became hung up in my porch rails. The ribs are fairly flexible and animals can squeeze them through some tight openings, but the hips are rigid. After finding resistance at the hips the animal attempts to back up, but the ribs would have flared back out and the animal would be trapped at the waist.

I went back to my truck, got a heavy blanket and approached the buck from the front. He stared at me in wide-eyed alarm but was too exhausted to struggle much as I covered his head and sharp hooves with the blanket. It was a challenge to squeeze the rib cage together while pushing up and back, but fortunately he wasn't very big and in seconds he rallied his strength and somersaulted over backwards onto the deck and leapt to his feet. I then stared in horror as he bolted down the deck on a high-speed collision course with Mr. Lockwood. The old man took one look and reversed direction faster than I thought possible, tapping along with his walker while images of catastrophe flooded my mind. Surely he would be seriously injured, even killed. Why hadn't I asked him to stand farther back or go inside the house? Thankfully, Mr. Lockwood made a rapid turn to the right, toward his front door, while the deer shot left and away to the safety of the trees.

A similar call involving a big doe caught in a wrought iron gate came in early on a Monday morning. The homeowner sounded terribly disturbed when I advised him by phone that I was on my way. "You can't get anywhere near her," he said. "She just goes crazy!"

"Stay away from her and I'll be there as soon as I can," I told him.

It was one of those bright beautiful mornings when it seems unfair to be paid to be driving around this gorgeous county. I steered the truck higher and higher up the wooded hillside with views of the valley below and pulled up to the elegant estate about fifteen minutes later. The caller waved at me from the window of the Spanish-style mansion and motioned that he would be right down. The doe was firmly wedged in the heavy iron gate and she struggled wildly as I approached with my blanket. I continued to slowly advance and she finally gave up, resigned to her fate as I covered her head and squeezed her ribs together using both hands. The moment she could, she yanked away from me and was free and out of sight in the nearby forest in seconds. The rescue had taken maybe two minutes total.

I folded my blanket and had just replaced it in the truck when the man and his wife walked down to meet me dressed in bathrobes and slippers. Looking around in surprise, the man said, "Where's the deer?"

"I let her go."

"But how did you do it?" He was stumped.

I explained my technique while the woman looked on with her hand covering her mouth in shock. She finally recovered her poise enough to say, "We thought you were going to have to shoot her and cut her up in pieces."

I laughed at the thought of unnecessary carnage and in this beautiful setting. I could just see myself grimly hacking the poor creature apart and setting chunks of flesh in the expensive landscaping as blood poured down the hill. Their relief and gratefulness tickled me as we chatted for a few minutes with the sun flooding the hillside and the valley spreading below us.

Fortunately, big mature bucks don't get caught in fences like this because they can't fit through with their antlers in the first place. Antlers do cause other problems, though, as bucks are always getting them hung up in a variety of places. Two fellow officers responded to a call once of a buck tangled up by one antler in a badminton net. When they arrived, the animal was leaping around violently and waving his tangled antlers threateningly at anyone who came near. He was far too powerful to safely attempt a takedown with a blanket, so discussion ensued about how best to address the issue. Finally, it was decided that the only way to do a long distance rescue was to attempt to shoot through the antler and free him that way. One of the officers sighted down the barrel of the rifle and in one perfect shot relieved the buck of the offending antler and kept it for a souvenir while the deer, free at last from his dilemma, bolted for the forest with his mismatched rack.

I once had a yearling buck that was tangled by both small antlers in a

144

batting cage. He had managed to rip some of the netting free, which gave him a range of about twenty feet and he could gallop around like a horse on a long line, panting in terror. Thankfully, he was small enough that I was able to rein him in with the netting while fending off his lunges at me with a thick comforter. I tackled him and held him down while cutting through the netting with my pocket knife.

And it isn't only antlers that get tangled in netting. Another time, a small spotted fawn got a front leg tangled in a child's goalie netting in a residential backyard. The worried resident had attempted to free the baby without luck, so I was called out. Fawns are among the most adorable of babies and this creature looked up at me with its huge brown eyes while I cut a circle of netting free and then unwrapped the tiny leg. I attempted to make the baby stand to make sure it had use of the limb, but it sank straight down each time. I realized then it was following mom's instructions to lie still and wait for her. There was no sign of mama but deer often leave their babies for extended periods when they are very young and I suspected she would be back. I massaged the limb for a few more moments and then tucked the baby into some long grass nearby, advising the resident to let me know if it was still there the next day. A phone call an hour or so later confirmed that mama had come for her baby.

Our county is very fortunate to have a wonderful fawn rescue, so when I got a call of a baby huddled next to its dead mother on the side of a busy freeway I was able to scoop it up and call for help. The woman who runs fawn rescue is a dynamic and dedicated senior who has cared for orphaned and injured fawns for as long as anyone can remember. She's at an age when many of her counterparts have either long since passed away or are being spoon-fed in a care facility. She has no time for that. The babies need her and she keeps on working tirelessly to save them. She met me halfway so I didn't have to drive all the way to her rescue and I again marveled at her commitment. We chatted for a moment about the fawn and then transferred it gently to her vehicle. I watched her drive away thinking that the world needs more people like her.

Another common hazard for deer and other wildlife are backyard swimming pools. Especially in the summer months when other sources of water dry up, animals often attempt to drink out of in-ground pools and tumble in. Pools with steps are usually easy as we can guide the animal toward the steps and let it climb out on its own. But some pools have ladder-style stairs and are much harder for wildlife and rescuers alike.

Officer Dave Birch arrived to assist me on one such call in the heat of August. The deer was swimming anxious circles in the clear blue water of the caller's swimming pool, occasionally attempting unsuccessfully to lunge out of her watery trap. It would have been easy enough to throw a rope over her head and pull her out, but I knew from experience about the problem of getting the rope off the panicked animal once it was out of the water. It's a good way to injure both deer and people.

Dave and I decided to stretch a rope across the pool and use it to push the deer into a corner and then pull her out with it. Our plan proceeded flawlessly in spite of her attempts to leap over or duck under the rope. We had even thought ahead to direct her to the corner nearest the open gate to send her out of the yard completely. But things went awry when we lifted her out and pointed her toward the gate. As soon as she leapt to her feet, instead of exiting the yard, she went zinging around it, missing her escape route completely. The best thing for us to do would have been to leave her alone and let her find her way out on her own but the resident needed to shut the gate so he could let his dog out into the yard. We quietly maneuvered back and forth, trying to herd her out of the yard while she raced around, sailing over a cluster of whimsical garden gnomes, nearly falling back into the pool and then crashing behind a shed. She rocketed out from behind the shed sporting a stack of tomato cages on her head. As she continued her charge her legs became entangled in the wire of the tomato cages and she stumbled to the ground. We had to tackle the poor girl to remove the wire and she finally bolted out of the gate and was gone.

26. What Was I Thinking?

In the dim glow of a distant streetlight, the seriousness of my situation was beginning to dawn on me. The faces of the five gang members showed intense hostility as they surrounded me, demanding their dogs back. I was starting to wonder at the wisdom of entering the mean part of town, by myself, late at night, to deal with a dog attack. I had left Luci home tonight and I was feeling pretty alone. My heart hammered in my chest as they drew closer, arguing and insisting that I release the dogs. The two dogs had attacked a man and sent him to the hospital, but they hadn't given me any trouble and were already safely locked in the truck. I could see a bulge in the pocket of one of the men. I knew without a doubt he wasn't glad to see me, which left the possibility of a gun.

The police officer, who arrived after the initial 911 call, spoke to me by phone and said he would be leaving the scene but that the dog owner knew I was coming and was being compliant. I wasn't happy to hear the officer was leaving. It was late and this was one of the scarier neighborhoods in the area, a hotbed of crime and gang activity. Still, I didn't want to look like a wuss, I mean, what a baby, asking for backup just because I'm a blonde woman going to a gang-infested ghetto. *Wimp.* Besides, these things usually turn out okay. I bit my lip and didn't ask him to stay.

Not my best move.

I hadn't been too worried when I first arrived because the dog owner, a young man, was reasonable and gave me no trouble. I didn't know yet how serious the attack was. The victim had been transported to the hospital by ambulance, but that didn't always mean much. I had once seen a man with a puncture to the hand by a miniature poodle taken away by ambulance. I explained to the dog owner that the dogs would need to be quarantined at the shelter but that he might be able to get them back after the quarantine and an investigation. The man had loaded up the dogs for me. The muscular black and white male and brindle female jumped into the truck at his request and didn't even give me a look. He said he really wanted to get his male dog, Tyrone, back as he had never had any trouble with him. He had taken in the other dog, Nera , recently because her owners didn't want her because of her aggression. She was only a year old but had already shown some ugly reactions to both people and other animals.

I had been trying to finish up my paperwork and get out of there but the dog owner had a number of reasonable questions about the process and what he needed to do. The trouble started when a group of men pulled up in a truck. They got out and surrounded us, demanding to know what was going on and why I was taking their homies dogs. One of them was up in my face demanding the dogs back while several of the others started messing around on the far side of my truck where I couldn't see them. I heard them calling to the dogs. "Tyrone, come on, man, here boy, come here, Tyrone." The dogs began to whine and scratch inside my truck.

"Please stop that, you're upsetting them," I called out.

148

"Man, you the one upsettin' them, Miss Animal Control, locking them in a cage." They yelled at me in taunting voices while continuing to call to the dogs. Almost before I could respond, the truck began rocking and I realized they were yanking on the dog-box door handle with all their strength.

"Get back from the truck!" I commanded, trying to sound tougher than I felt. I jumped in the truck and started it up. I could see the men in my mirrors on all sides of the vehicle. The truck was rocking violently by then and I threw it in gear and gunned it out of there, not caring if I ran over a few of them in the process. The truck bounced over the edge of the curb as I careened onto the main road. I looked back at the dog-box doors in the side view mirrors and I could see they were safely shut. I gave a silent thanks to Jim, my training officer, the one who taught me to always lock the doors when anything was put inside.

I had almost stopped hyperventilating by the time I arrived at the hospital emergency room to interview my victim. The unfortunate man was covered in injuries from head to toe. He had a nasty abrasion on his forehead where he had hit it during his fall and there were dog bites all over his body — arms, legs, torso, everywhere. None of the individual bites was terrible, it was that there were just so many of them. I asked him what had happened as I began to photograph the injuries.

The poor man was clearly traumatized, and he told his story in broken English. The two dogs had been in the backyard when he had parked near their gate to visit the duplex next door. The dogs had been barking at him through the fence and started slamming up against the gate. When the latch suddenly gave way, the dogs had such momentum they were propelled into the alley. The man had taken a look at the two big dogs roaring at him and was off and running at top speed. Unfortunately, not even an Olympic sprinter could have outrun these dogs.

The dogs overtook him halfway across the driveway. They were so fired up by the chase they had knocked him down and bitten him from head to toe in the few seconds before the owner heard the commotion and ran out to grab his dogs and drag them back to the house by their collars. The victim had been left moaning on the ground while his friends called 911.

When I got home that night I spilled my story to Paul. "You should have racked your shotgun!" he reprimanded. We both laughed at the image of Blondie chasing off a bunch of terrified gang members with a shotgun.

"Yeah, I should have shot off a few rounds. That would have fixed them." But Paul turned serious again. "You shouldn't have gone on that call without police backup."

"I know, I know. I'll be more careful next time." I knew he was right. It's just too easy for things to go wrong.

The owner claimed his male dog after quarantine, with numerous fees and restrictions imposed. He surrendered the female and she was euthanized. Sadly, she was far too big and aggressive to safely adopt out.

27. Held Hostage by Wildlife

The noise pierced my dreams, drawing me from the fog of sleep as I struggled to place the sound. It seemed quite close, a cheery repetitive beat that went on and on. Of course. My cell phone. I glanced at the time as I reached for it. 11:25 p.m. Ugh. I had been asleep for less than half an hour.

I tried not to disturb Paul as I whispered "hello" into the phone. The police dispatcher sounded entirely too chipper for this time of night; there was probably something wrong with her. She cheerfully described a caller on Apple Creek Lane who had a raccoon in her apartment. At least a raccoon in a house is a fairly common problem and usually one I can resolve over the phone.

I sat up in bed and dialed the number. A hysterical young woman who sounded ready to climb straight up a wall answered on the first ring. She started screaming into the phone. "Oh my God, there's a raccoon in my house, it's in the hall right outside my bedroom, I'm so scared, I'm here alone with my daughter, oh my God, you have to do something!"

I had to cut in at that point because I had a feeling that she could go on for a long time. "Ma'am, what's your name?"

"It's Amber, please, you have to help me!"

"Amber, how did the raccoon get into your house?" I guessed she had a cat door.

"I leave the sliding door open for my cats."

It took me a moment to process this information in my sleepy state. I must have misunderstood her. Surely no one would leave their door open on Apple Creek Lane. Apple Creek was one of the scariest little streets in our whole jurisdiction. The murder capital of the county, gang central, drugs, crime, you name it. I double checked with her to be sure I heard her right. Yes, she definitely left her door ajar, with cat food right inside. You might as well put up a neon sign saying, "Welcome raccoons." But never mind that, it was the people in the neighborhood that I was worried about.

I was wide awake by then, afraid someone would come in her door and rape and rob her while we were talking. She would be better off just closing the animals inside as long as her door was shut, padlocked, braced with two-by-fours and booby-trapped. There had been a gang murder on that street just the month before. The wildlife in that area was probably packing heat for all I knew. I shook my head to dispel the image of a small masked bandit gripping a pistol in his little furry paws as he shook my caller down for her cat food. "Hand over the Meow Mix in a brown paper bag and no one gets hurt."

The woman's screams snapped me back to attention. "Oh, my God, now there's two of them, you have to do something! I just looked out and now there are two and they're looking right at me and eating my cat's food!"

"Amber, do you have a broom or a mop or anything you can bang around and chase them back out the door with, or anything really noisy you can use?"

"No, everything like that is in the kitchen, I don't have anything in here!"

"Try yelling and throwing something, like a pillow or your purse, at them."

152

"No, they won't leave. When I crack the door open to look out they just look right at me."

At that moment I heard the small voice of the daughter in the background. "Mommy, I'm scared."

Amber's voice then filled the air in one long scream. I held the phone away from my ear. I was sure I'd be able to hear her screaming at her daughter from across town even if I hung up. "QUIT FREAKING OUT, YOU AREN'T HELPING, YOU JUST NEED TO CALM DOWN AND STOP BEING A SPAZ!" she yelled at the top of her lungs.

I cut in again at that point, yelling over Amber's voice. "AMBER, STOP YELLING AT YOUR DAUGHTER."

Paul started up in bed, thrashing and looking around wildly as I hollered into the phone. I turned to see him glaring at me bleary-eyed in the pale glow of the digital clock. "Sorry, sweetie," I whispered, lowering my voice on the phone now that I had Amber's attention. "Amber, you need to calm down and comfort your daughter, you're upsetting her."

At that point I heard Amber's surprised response. "Oh wow, they're gone. I just looked out and the raccoons are gone."

I wasn't surprised. After all that hysteria the local gang members had probably fled the area, too. "Amber," I said, "you need to check and make sure they are gone and then close and lock your door."

"But one of my cats is still outside."

Are you kidding, I thought. Never mind the cats, babe, your life is at stake out there. Paul turned over in bed and covered his head with a pillow. I tried to whisper into the phone. "Amber, you need to close your door. You can let your cat in tomorrow morning." I didn't mention that her cat shouldn't be outside at all in that neighborhood or some homie might be feeding it to his dog. I said goodnight to Amber amid her protests and snuggled up against Paul. Miraculously, he didn't throw me off the bed for disturbing him. He wrapped his arms around me and drifted back to sleep.

Most of the time we can advise people on how to deal with these types of problems themselves, but occasionally we do respond, depending on the circumstances. I will always assist an elderly or disabled person if needed, but I can be frustrated by the failure of perfectly capable people to deal with simple wildlife issues. The women in my own family are noted for being very capable. My great-grandmother would have probably shot and skinned any trespassing wildlife and served it for dinner. My grandmothers on both sides would have chased away anything from opossums to bears with a broom and a few no-nonsense shouts. My mom would have gently rescued anything that needed rescuing, but any creature that gave her trouble would have been knocked into the next county.

With that kind of upbringing it's no wonder I am occasionally baffled by people's unwillingness to at least attempt to take care of their own problems. One man, John, called 911 at 2:30 a.m. saying he had three and maybe even four raccoons in his house. He was pretty panicked. Raccoons are usually fairly solitary, so it was most likely a mom with her young or a group of adolescent siblings. His was a similar situation of leaving the sliding door open and cat food inside. Raccoons are nothing if not opportunistic. I tried to explain how to get behind them and make a big aggressive racket and chase them out the door. He whined and fussed and tried to get me to come and do it for him, but he lived forty minutes away and I was exhausted. I felt like asking to speak to the man of the house, but I bit my tongue and continued trying to talk him through it. I tried to build him up and help him be brave. Raccoons can be ferocious if cornered, but these probably weighed less than twenty pounds apiece and they were in his territory. I could hear his pitiful attempts at following my instructions in the background.

"Shoo, go on, shoo," he practically whispered, and I could hear him tapping a pan lid with a small utensil. I could just picture the cocky young raccoons glancing up and then going back to their business of ransacking his house, totally unconcerned. "JOHN," I yelled into the phone. (Heck, maybe if I yelled loud enough maybe I could scare them off from my end.) "YOU NEED TO GET SERIOUS! SOUND LIKE YOU MEAN IT!"

He tried again, banging his pan lid a little harder. "Go on, get out of here."

Geez, I thought, he might as well make them some popcorn and stay up and watch a movie with them.

"JOHN! QUIT MESSING AROUND! THIS IS YOUR HOUSE, YOUR TURF, TAKE IT BACK, MAN. RUN THOSE LITTLE SUCKERS OFF. I WANT TO BE ABLE TO HEAR YOU FROM MY HOUSE EVEN IF I HANG UP THE PHONE!"

Apparently John could be taught, or maybe he just got mad enough, because I heard a tremendous crash, then "GET THE HELL OUT OF MY HOUSE YOU LITTLE BASTARDS. GET OUT, GET OOOOOOUUUUUUUT!" A series of crashes followed. It sounded like every pot, pan and utensil — and maybe even the microwave — had been hurled at the offending wildlife. Then I heard, "DAMN YOU! GET OUT OF MY HOUSE!" and a few more crashes. I thought I heard the sound of breaking glass but I couldn't be sure. And then all was quiet.

I waited on the line for a moment. "John? Are you there?"

There was the sound of heavy breathing and then John's deep voice. "They're gone." He sounded empowered, manly. He had conquered the enemy, protected his loved ones, taken back his home.

"Good job!"

In the case of a woman in a wheelchair with a full-grown raccoon in her house and her two big dogs trying to tear through a wall to get at it, I decided I'd better intervene. The dogs had chased the animal into the bathroom and she had closed the bathroom door, so I advised her to confine her dogs to the bedroom and I headed out. The raccoon had entered through the dog door in the back door, so when I arrived I opened it and shut all the other doors in the house. The woman positioned herself in the living room, out of the path of departure and I cautiously opened the bathroom door and peered in. The raccoon was a big male. He was standing on the sink and when he saw me he raised up on his hind legs, puffed up his fur so he looked like a giant hairy gorilla and growled deeply at me. Due to his position on the sink he was as tall as me, and he glared into my eyes. The bummer was that I would need to pass him in order to get behind him to chase him out.

I took a deep breath and flattened myself against the opposite wall in an attempt to ease past him in the narrow space. Slowly, I began to inch my way along, trying to be as unthreatening as possible. Raccoons rarely attack people but they are ferocious fighters when cornered and he was definitely cornered. I tried not to think of the proximity of his sharp teeth to my jugular as I worked my way behind him. He huffed and growled and threatened to make mincemeat out of my face, but finally I was behind him. I took out my asp and banged it against the sink. "GO ON, GET! GET HOME! He shot out the bathroom door and down the hall at high speed and I saw the flash of a furry rump and ringed tail rocket out the back door.

Skunks in houses are a little trickier. One wrong move and you're staying at the Holiday Inn for the next six weeks.

I like skunks. As a rule they mind their own business, they eat slugs and snails and other garden pests, and they're quiet and adorable. It's true, my dogs have been sprayed a few times and I didn't find them quite as adorable then. Especially the time I was eight months pregnant and we had a glass-sided corner shower, no tub. My husband came home to find me, my huge belly, and a very stinky eighty-pound Wolfhound crammed in the shower together. Would you believe the dear man laughed at me?

A woman with a baby skunk in her bedroom at ten o'clock at night called when I was working standby. It seemed like it would take longer to explain to her all the little nuances of non-odiferous skunk removal than to just do it myself, so I told her I was on my way. Besides, I wanted to see the little guy.

When I walked up the front sidewalk one of his brothers ambled past. A family of skunks obviously lived in the area. The caller, Angela, answered the door gratefully and escorted me in. She explained that she had left her bedroom sliding door open for a while that evening to cool off the house. When she was ready for bed she had closed and locked the door and then made her way toward the bathroom. Her little black and white kitten, Porky, had scurried past her as she walked by, but then she realized that Porky was on the bed. Looking back in surprise, she saw the little skunk scratching frantically against the sliding door, his escape route cut off.

Angela seemed like a sensible woman but she was understandably hesitant to take on this potential stink bomb in the room where she slept every night. I told her there were no guarantees and quietly opened the door to the master bedroom, hoping I wasn't going to ruin her day and mine. I couldn't see the skunk, but Porky was staring so intently at the curtain over the sliding glass door I had no doubt where the intruder was. As I moved further into the room I could see that the little guy was in the track next to the glass, and he was fussing back and forth anxiously trying to get out. Meanwhile, Porky, who was thrilled to have a new friend, batted playfully at the black and white striped tail. The two animals were of similar size and color and I hoped that the visitor was not offended by the kitten's interference. But he didn't take much notice of either the kitten or of me in his single-minded quest to be reunited with his mama.

I couldn't open the door all the way because the skunk was in the track, so I started to slide it very slowly and carefully. The little guy ignored me and continued his scramble as I used the door to coax him aside. I kept an eye on the tail the whole time. A skunk's tail is a great indicator of his mood. Naturally carried low, it will rise in the presence of a threat. After a moment I had the door most of the way open and I maneuvered myself behind him. Seconds later he found his way out the door to freedom, much to Porky's disappointment.

28. Are You Serious?

I don't usually answer the phones at work but I was covering for a clerk when the call came in. "I need to make a complaint about the way my neighbor treats his dog." The woman's voice on the phone was heavy with concern.

"What's the problem, ma'am?"

"I've watched this all winter without calling, but I just can't bear it anymore."

"What exactly is your neighbor doing to his dog?" I asked, while images of a poor neglected canine, huddling in the rain on the end of a chain, flitted through my head.

"It's just not fair," she continued. "This is a big beautiful black Lab and he deserves better treatment."

"Can you explain the situation for me?" I prodded.

"You have to understand this dog is only a year old, and it happens constantly!"

Okay, I wasn't getting anywhere. I changed tactics. "What exactly is the violation of the law here?'

"It may not be a violation of the law, but it is still wrong!" she exclaimed.

"I can't investigate a complaint without knowing what we are looking for, ma'am. I need some details."

"Okay, the owner is in his forties. He moved in around three or four years ago. He's tall with brown hair and a mustache."

Wow! We were having a distinct communication problem here. "What's the problem? How is the dog being mistreated?!" I feared I was nearly yelling at this point in my effort to get to the bottom of this.

"Every day he takes the dog for a walk and it doesn't matter what the weather is or how cold or wet it is outside. HE WALKS HIS DOG IN THE RAIN!"

A Labrador? Getting wet? Tragic.

This is an example of some of the silly stuff we deal with every day. A lot of time is wasted on these types of things, but they can be amusing as well. One call sounded legitimate the way it came in. The reporting party stated there were multiple neglected cats, never fed and living in filth. I had been on plenty of calls like this and I could already picture it: a bunch of scrawny, goopy-eyed, sickly cats and kittens, reproducing at will, surrounded by garbage and feces. When I arrived I was surprised to find a tidy apartment with four fat, shiny cats lounging around comfortably on the furniture. It turned out the caller was the college student roommate of the cat owner. He showed me around. His complaint was that the pet owner never filled the cat food bowls, so he had to do it. The roommate didn't clean the litter box, either, which the man pointed out in a corner. It was indeed filthy, overflowing with feces, and there were several piles of feces on the floor where the cats, unable to bear stepping into the box, had relieved themselves on the carpet.

"Since the cats are healthy I can't really do about the litter box," I said, glancing at the four chubby felines. They could benefit from missing a meal. "It's not against the law to be a slob."

"But he's twenty-two years old. He should be taking care of his own cats, I shouldn't have to do it," the man complained.

"This is a civil issue between you and him. Maybe you could find a new living arrangement," I said.

"I can't afford anything else. Can't you just write him a warning or something?"

I felt kind of silly but it couldn't hurt; besides, I supposed it was a sanitation issue and certainly the cats would be better off with a clean litter box. I wrote: "To avoid a possible citation for sanitation the cat box must be scooped daily and litter changed weekly." The citation part was a stretch but the young man was tickled with his little warning notice, which I'm sure would be displayed in the cat owner's face the moment he walked in the door. The department has had a few calls very similar to this one and we always jokingly refer to them as cat crap calls.

The neglected horse call was rather vague and I read over the memo several times trying to make sense of it. It stated: "Horses look neglected, have blank looks on their faces." When someone says that an animal looks neglected, the clerks always ask for details. Is it thin? No shelter? Lack of food, water or necessary veterinary care? In this case the clerks couldn't get much more. I got a chuckle out of that, I mean, horses usually look like they're contemplating the universe or doing algebra in their heads just for fun.

I drove out and looked at the three horses, easily visible from the road. They were nice-looking quarter horses, two sorrels and a bay, resting under a spreading oak and they appearing utterly content standing head to tail in relaxed enjoyment, swishing the occasional fly. There was plenty of grazing available and a full trough of water nearby. The horses were of excellent weight and health and the hooves were neatly trimmed. As I gazed at them I realized that they did have blank looks on their faces, but it was siesta time; nobody runs around looking excited all the time. I would have to say I've seen humans parked in front of a television set showing less animation than these horses showed.

I wondered how much the caller knew about horses. But I appreciated her concern. If someone isn't sure there is a problem it's better to call just in

160

case. Still, I was dying to call her and say something like, "Hi, this is Shirley from animal control. I just wanted to let you know it turns out these horses practice Zen meditation every day at the exact time you drive by." Or "Those particular horses are just concentrating on quantum physics." Instead, I called and let her know the horses were very well cared for. She was happy to know they were okay.

Another horse call really made me do a double take when I read the memo. It said: "Skinny horse, eye swollen, pussy looks neglected." Whoa! This was a new one. I wasn't sure what my responsibility was regarding the last part. I could see the clerk had been trying to write that the eye was pus-sy, that is, that there was pus coming out of it, but the problem is you can't write the word "pussy" with the meaning "to have pus coming from it" without it coming out "pussy," especially with the comma where it was. I shared a laugh about it with the vet techs in the clinic. One of the techs, an attractive single woman of about thirty, stopped laughing long enough to say, quite seriously, "Never mind the horse, what about mine? I haven't been laid in two years!" That brought more hysterical laughter, and jokes about slacker stallions and the lack of enough good men to go around.

We also get a lot of calls about horses lying down. Horses do lie down, people! Especially if the weather has been bad for a few days. When the sun comes out, it seems like every old horse in the county lies down and we can't convince people that the poor old thing is just resting and enjoying the sun. No, they insist, you don't understand. It's lying flat out, something is really wrong! I then have to drive halfway across the county, where, in most cases the horse is already up. But if it's not, heaven help us, because I have to go out there and make the poor old thing get up just to be sure. In cases where the horse really is down and in distress it is rarely just lying there. Usually that horse is struggling to rise or breathing heavily or showing other signs that something is amiss and this can be seen even at a distance.

A call about a herd of cows without food or water had me surveying a pasture of knee-high grass in confusion. The group of yearlings was in good

161

weight and had around forty acres of excellent grazing available. There was a large trough of clean water with an automatic valve to keep it filled. There were even fish in it to control mosquitoes. The field was next to a busy freeway, so I supposed that of the thousands of people who drive by every day there might be one who doesn't know what cows eat. Maybe they thought we should whip up some pancakes for them, or a hot bowl of chili with cornbread.

How about this one? "Hello, Animal Control. How can I help you?"

"Yes, I was just at the Chinese restaurant, you know, the one downtown on Third Street? Well, anyway, you know how Chinese restaurants always have a tank of fish by the cash register, like it's the law or something?"

"Yes, so what's the problem?"

"Well...I think the tank has too many fish for how big it is."

We'll get right on that.

Sometimes the descriptions people give are unique all by themselves. "Yeah, hi. I was just at Canfield Park and I saw a Russian lady with big lips kicking a cocker spaniel." So I'm driving around the park looking at people's lips. Nope, too small, oh, here's one with big lips, but she's walking a Lhasa Apso. And what does a Russian lady look like anyway? And what do I do if I locate Ms. Big Lips? I'm going to check out her dog but as long as he looks okay, no injuries or shoe marks or anything, I can't do much. "Hi, I'm Shirley from Animal Control, have you been kicking your dog?"

"I would never do that!"

"Thank you. Have a good day."

Of course I want every animal, even goldfish, to have the best life they can. It's just that there's only so much I can do about some of the calls we get and I always do try to educate people as much as possible.

One woman was grievously disappointed in me because I let her down when she needed help with her cat issue. It seems that Marion had gone away for a few days and her house sitter had not seen one of her cats, Tommy, during that time. It's not unusual for felines to boycott their digs for a while if the owner is gone. On Marion's return she immediately posted signs about her lost pet. A neighbor named Theresa called. She lived across the street and a few doors down. Tommy had shown up at Theresa's house and she had been feeding him until she saw the poster and made this call. Marion picked up Tommy and thanked Theresa profusely. End of story.

Except that Tommy decided life with Theresa suited him better than life with Marion. Every time Tommy went outside he would head straight to Theresa's and Marion would go over and drag him home. This went on for a week or two until Marion got fed up and called us. Animal control is not meant to handle matters of kitty custody and I attempted to explain this to Marion on the phone.

"I am sorry, ma'am, but this is a civil issue between you and your neighbor," I said.

"But my cat could get killed by a car crossing the road to go back to her house!"

"Then I suggest you confine your cat to the house," I advised.

"I can't keep him in! He darts out the door every time I open it."

"You're smarter than he is. Check for him before you open the door." The smarter part was debatable, but surely one adult human could figure out a way to keep a cat in the house. Actually, I could commiserate because of my declawed and brain-injured cat James who darts out the door every chance he gets.

"But she feeds him when he's there, so he keeps going back," she whined. "Can't you tell her not to feed him?"

"Ma'am, it's her house. She can put chopped steak on her porch if she wants. You are allowing your cat to trespass onto her property." I was starting to lose patience by then; I had other more pressing calls to attend to. This woman had a stronger personality than mine, though, and she continued to wear me down.

"And besides, she has a cat door so Tommy can just go right in. I asked her to lock it but she flat out refuses. You need to tell her she has to lock her cat door."

163

"She is not required to lock her cat door."

"But she doesn't even have a cat!" Marion wailed.

"Your choices are to confine your cat, continue to go get him and put him at risk going back across the road, or just let him stay there."

"I can't leave him there, he's mine."

"Marion, why do you think your cat wants to stay there?" I was starting to get it just from talking to her but wanted her take on it.

"Well, we have two other cats that kind of pick on him, but he belongs with me. I've had him since he was a kitten."

"It's no wonder he wants to leave. Have you considered respecting what Tommy wants?"

There was a long pause. I had hoped I was getting through, but she came back with more of the same. "Can't you just talk to her? I even bought the woman a can of cat repellent but she won't even open the door or answer her phone now." Jeez, I thought, it's no wonder. The poor woman probably feels like she's being stalked.

I finally agreed to talk to Theresa, as a courtesy, if only to get Marion off my back. I even agreed to deliver the cat repellent but would not force its use. When I arrived at Theresa's attractive home, she came out to discuss the situation with me. A cheerful, down-to-earth woman with brunette waves streaked with gray, she explained that when the cat, who she called Buzz, had first shown up at her house she thought he was dumped and had begun feeding him. Now he expected it. She had gladly relinquished him to Marion initially but when he kept returning, she had to wonder why. I don't believe that Tommy/Buzz was mistreated, just that he preferred to be the only cat, not unusual.

Theresa had started getting concerned when she came home from the store one day to find Marion on her knees looking through the cat door on her back deck. She asked Marion not to trespass, but it continued to happen, so she got a lock for her gate. I showed her the cat repellent and she laughed and said she really needed some Marion repellent instead. She took the can but told me she didn't want to use it and I explained she didn't have to.

If only our calls just dealt with animals it would be a lot simpler. I had never even seen the cat in this case and between phone calls and visits dealing with the situation I had spent several hours on it. A great use of taxpayer money.

Some calls sound a lot worse than they really are. You may already have noticed: People use the word "attacked" rather freely. I have had people call and say they were attacked by a dog when all it did was bark at them from twenty feet away. One case, though, sounded really serious. The man's voice on the phone was panicked when he was transferred through from 911. "Oh, my God, we have a man being attacked here. There's three of them, please hurry!" He sounded so desperate I was sure these must be some really aggressive dogs. I grabbed Dave as he walked by and pointed urgently to the screen where I was typing up the call from dispatch.

"Where are you, sir?" I said, anxious to get an officer started.

"We're at the Redwood Campground. You have to hurry."

I typed it in and Dave hurried out the door.

"What happened?" I asked the caller. "Do you need an ambulance?"

"A man was swimming in the river and they came after him totally unprovoked and they just won't stop. They're all over him. You have to hurry, they won't stop."

"What kind of dogs are they?" I asked.

"They aren't dogs," he replied. "They're geese, three of them."

Geese? Are you kidding me? Geese can be aggressive and they can give a nasty pinch with their beaks. They might even whack you with their big wings or chase you across the lawn, but they're geese. They don't have teeth or claws and they weigh less than the average cocker spaniel. If necessary, even a child can grab a goose by the neck and restrain it. Let me tell you, if you grabbed one of those sassy things and held it under water for just a second it would cool its jets pretty quick.

29. Never a Dull Moment

I enjoy the variety that comes with being an animal control officer. Sometimes we get the same old loose dog calls for a while but then come the unique calls to break it up. When I overheard a call dispatched to Jim for a "big lizard" I immediately offered to take it. Jim doesn't care for reptiles but I love the challenge. Jim said he would meet me there. Nice. He doesn't want to handle the beast but he wants to watch me do it.

"Big lizard" can mean anything from a little blue-belly to an iguana, and we do get quite a few iguana calls, so that was the most likely scenario. But Jim and I had a big surprise awaiting us. Standing in the driveway was a five-foot-long, carnivorous Nile Monitor lizard. A five-foot Nile Monitor is much larger and more aggressive than a five-foot Iguana. They stand taller and are heavier bodied with lots of sharp teeth and a ferocious disposition. This one, it turned out, had escaped from a nearby reptile rescue facility when a volunteer had failed to latch the cage correctly.

This was my first time dealing with a Nile Monitor, but I relied on what I knew about handling large snakes and reptiles. I slipped on some heavy gloves and slowly approached the animal. The closer I got the more the lizard curled his head and tail at me in a threat display. Eyes steady on me, he drew back his tail in an almost complete circle. He was going to let me have it any minute. Whack! As I lunged for his head, the tail whipped a lightning-quick strike to my leg. I felt the blow through my pants but my heavy high boots cut most of the sting out of it. I had him right behind the head with one hand while the other tried to hold the wildly struggling body. A big mouthful of teeth attempted to bite me through the ferocious wrestling match that followed. Finally, he quieted in my hands, glaring balefully at the world as Jim grinned at me from twenty feet away. The facility quickly claimed the mammoth reptile, but it made for an interesting day.

A call of a cat that had entered a resident's yard and been attacked by his dogs seemed average enough until I got there and saw what I was dealing with. The cat had come over the fence into the man's yard and his dogs went after it. The caller said the cat was injured and hiding behind his tool shed. I caught a glimpse of his dogs through the sliding glass door as we headed for the yard. The yellow Lab and the Pit mix both had bloody faces and the Lab had a lacerated ear. At first I thought the blood must have been from the unfortunate cat but on closer inspection I could see a network of nasty scratches and bloody furrows across the muzzles of both dogs. That must have been one tough kitty, I thought. I wondered how badly it was injured.

I walked behind the shed and caught a glimpse of spotted fur beneath some tall weeds. As I got closer a large, long muzzled face turned toward me and hissed long and loudly, followed by an ominous growl. A Savannah cat! These wildcat hybrids are larger than house cats and many retain some of their wild ancestry in their behavior. They have gorgeous spotted coats and are taller and longer than regular cats with exotic-looking faces. Savannah cats are becoming more popular as exotic house pets and we had started to see them occasionally both as strays and surrendered. This was no ordinary kitty, and he didn't appear to have a mark on him.

Even your average house cat can be hard to handle after a traumatic experience and this animal was extremely cranky. I managed to net him and get him into a cage with his long limbs flailing and his sleek, spotted coat glistening over powerful muscles. It looked like the dogs had gotten the worst end of that deal.

The frantic owners showed up at the shelter later that day to claim their cat. They had paid $5,000 for him and he wasn't allowed outside, they explained, but he had ripped through a screen that morning and gone prowling.

Most people don't realize what a problem hybrids can be. We occasionally get calls for wolf hybrids, as well. I recall seeing a wolf hybrid that lives at our local wildlife center. Sheila was probably mostly Siberian Husky but the length of muzzle and other features gave her away. She was very bonded to the director, and would hang out in her office all day, or frolic on the beach with her, but with strangers her demeanor was very wolfish. She slunk around, head and tail low, glancing out of the corner of her eye as she furtively tried to disappear. I always ignored her, so she didn't mind me. The director and I had even gone to the beach with Sheila and my dogs without issue, though she didn't always act like a dog.

Genetics can be interesting. The wildlife center had a tame coyote that often played with Sheila. The coyote, called Wiley, had been found as a pup by some people who thought he was a regular puppy and taken him in to the local Humane Society. He was so tame and people-friendly we knew he had been raised by humans. But he was a coyote, so the shelter transferred him to the wildlife center, where he was isolated from people except for the most necessary of care and handling. Still, the efforts made to treat Wiley like the coyote he was were futile. Wiley loved people and would run to any stranger and wag and lick like any Golden Retriever.

Most wild animals raised by humans stay suspicious of strangers and retain a lot of wild instinct as they mature. Wiley was temperamental and would bite like a crocodile if annoyed, but overall he loved people and could never be safely released because of it. He was around a year old when I first met him and had been neutered and made a part of the wildlife center's educational display

168

Wiley and Sheila were in a large outdoor enclosure together at the wildlife center when I stopped in one day. Wiley ran to greet me, yipping with excitement and leaping to try to lick me. Sheila slunk around the back of the enclosure surveying me suspiciously from behind the trees and brush. Wiley was 100 percent coyote and very friendly while Sheila was probably less than half wolf and highly suspicious. A fascinating display of genetics.

One gentleman in our county had a penchant for keeping ostriches and we had various problems with the huge birds over the years. The owner, Fred, didn't do a great job of confining the territorial animals, which sometimes resulted in catastrophe. Ostriches can stand eight feet tall and weigh over 300 pounds and they have some killer drumsticks. One kick from those muscular legs can be deadly. Officer Rich Owens had been forced to shoot one of them after it escaped from its pen and attacked several people. Several years later a neighbor entered the field where one of the ostriches, called Jerry, lived, to retrieve a Frisbee. Jerry kicked the stuffing out of her. The poor woman sustained a lacerated scalp, cracked ribs and internal injuries and spent a week in the hospital. Fred was asked to move Jerry to another location after that and, lacking a place of his own, he rented space in a well-thought-out location next to an elementary school. School officials were unimpressed with the sagging four-foot-high sheep fence around Jerry's new field and insisted he be relocated immediately.

Two days later I received a call of a loose ostrich in nearby Oak Hill and arrived on the scene to find the humongous tweety bird roaming a pasture behind the caller's home. The woman, who had been playing with her baby granddaughter in the backyard, had been decidedly unamused when an eight-foot-tall ostrich lumbered around the corner and headed straight for them. Who knows, maybe he just wanted a bite of the watermelon they were sharing on the lawn but she wasn't waiting to find out. Thankfully, she was able to grab the baby and dart inside and neither was mauled. The bird followed her to the sliding glass door where he pecked hopefully at the glass for a few minutes while she huddled inside fearing the panel would give way under its assault.

With the terrified woman corralled inside her house, the ostrich roamed the nearby pasture and I set about locating the owner. I suspected I was dealing with Jerry. I knew that Fred didn't live in that area but had probably found another field to rent nearby.

I kept a cautious eye out for Jerry as I went to the nearest house but no one was home. At the next house I was fortunate to find a helpful young woman who said the ostrich had been brought there the night before by a man named Fred something or other. I had never met Fred and asked for a description. I was intrigued by the one the woman gave me. Usually it's something like, "Well, he's about average height with brown hair and uh...that's all I remember." "He looks like Willie Nelson and he drives an old green pickup with a hound dog in the back," she said. "You just missed him. He pulled out of the other driveway right after you pulled in. I tried to flag him down but he was in a hurry." I bet he split in a hurry, I thought. He knows he's in big trouble for letting this dangerous animal escape yet again.

I spent the next half hour or so making sure Jerry didn't maul anyone or get onto the highway while calling around trying to track down his wayward owner. At the sound of a vehicle in the driveway that ran past the caller's house, I looked up to see Willie Nelson pull up in a green pickup with a hound dog in the back. Dang, I thought, that lady nailed it. Apparently old Willie, oops, I mean Fred, had decided he had better return and take responsibility for Jerry before the bird was blasted into the next county. I watched in wonder as he grabbed a can of creamed corn out of the truck and set off in the direction of Jerry's aimless wandering. "They will do anything for a can of creamed corn," he called over his shoulder. Yeah right, I thought, good luck with that. A few minutes later Fred returned with Jerry following and peering over his shoulder like a parakeet on steroids, hoping for another bite of creamed corn. Who knew?

When Officer Dave Birch was new to the job, he asked me to assist him on a call for an injured baby mountain lion. We do have mountain lions in our county, but it's extremely rare to get a call for one. "Where's it located?" I asked, skeptically. He named a street in the dead center of the tract section of

170

town, not even near a creek or any type of wildlife corridor. "It's just a feral cat, I'm sure, but I'll be glad to help you with it," I said, disappointed.

Dave followed me to the address, where the homeowner greeted us and led the way to his backyard. He pointed to the landscaping at the back. I walked up to the bushes and carefully peered in to find an adolescent bobcat snarling a fearsome warning. Wow! I had to admit I was impressed. Maybe not a mountain lion but certainly not what I was expecting.

The bobcat was quite a bit taller and longer than a house cat and was all skin and bones. I could see it had an injured leg. With a quick swoop, I had him netted and bundled into a cage, where he sliced at me with an impressive set of claws while Dave watched in amusement.

At the wildlife rescue center I helped a staff member do an intake exam. The animal was emaciated and dehydrated, so I held him carefully by the scruff of the neck while she administered subcutaneous fluids. I left the beautiful animal in the staff's capable hands and returned to work. The bobcat had surgery to repair the leg and was ultimately released in the remote wilderness.

The public doesn't tend to be educated about the local wildlife and we occasionally get a call for a baby bobcat that usually turns out to be a Manx kitten with the classic short stub of a tail. So when a man brought in a small shoebox with holes cut in it and said his kids had caught a baby bobcat, the technician on duty casually flipped up the lid expecting to see a house cat. She was greeted with a terrifying snarl from the unhappy resident. What do you know? It *was* a baby bobcat. Even that wasn't as bad as one officer who answered a call for a baby beaver all alone on a golf course. The rescuers had confined the poor infant in a box and were waiting for us anxiously. We don't have much in the way of beavers in this area here but there were ponds nearby and we've seen stranger things. The officer headed out to find an ordinary gopher gnashing his yellow teeth in frustration at his confinement.

Part of the challenge of my job can be finding creative ways to rescue animals in distress. A call of a bird in the fireplace one day had me brainstorming. The sparrow had somehow fallen down the chimney and landed on a small ledge inside. It was just high enough inside that I could neither see nor reach it. The residents had been trying to get to it for nearly an hour. I leaned in and shined my flashlight into the dark and the bird fluttered vainly upward only to fall back onto the ledge a few seconds later. I reached up into the sooty blackness with no luck, and it was too narrow to get any farther in. If only he would fall down into the fireplace I could grab him and take him outside. The bird made several more unsuccessful attempts at freedom, each time landing out of reach on the ledge. I tried to think of a way to get under him during one of his flying attempts and funnel him down into the fireplace. "Do you have any cardboard?" I asked the resident, thinking maybe I could slip it under the bird when he flew up and keep him from landing on the ledge. A moment later, the bird slid down the cardboard ramp and into my waiting hand to be released unharmed outside. Completely satisfying.

Another time a bird was trapped in a very narrow space at the back of the chimney of a wood stove. The reach was longer than my arm. I could see the poor thing in my flashlight beam, panting in distress. I needed something long and thin to could grab with. Remembering my success with the kittens in the barn, I ran out the truck for the tongs I had started carrying. A careful grasping of the bird with BBQ tongs had him out in seconds.

We have a lot of opossums in our county and get called for them frequently. They get injured by cars and dogs, stuck in weird places, and they wander into homes through pet doors. One nice gentleman called about a sick opossum in his yard. I arrived at his beautiful estate and was welcomed into the house. I admired the stunning view of the valley through the picture windows as we walked a few miles through the home to the back door. In the pool area he pointed out a young opossum ambling along the fence line in their usual random way. "He looks pretty healthy to me," I said. "They tend to be a little slow."

The man looked puzzled. "When I saw him this morning I tried to shoo him out with a broom and he kind of staggered around and then he fell over and just lay there like he was dead."

I paused for a moment, trying to think of how to say it, not wanting to

172

embarrass him. "They do that a lot; it's a defense mechanism called playing dead or playing opossum."

The man looked mortified and smacked his hand against his skull. "Playing opossum! Of course, I feel so silly. I'm so sorry to waste your time."

"It's really okay," I said. "It's a common mistake."

30. Mary Jane

A really sappy song came on the radio on my way home from work one day. It's called "The Christmas Shoes" and is about a little boy whose mother is dying. He wants to buy her a sparkly pair of shoes to wear to heaven. I was choked up and dripping tears so bad I could hardly drive. I marveled at the fact that I deal with neglect, abuse, cruelty and countless other sad things at work every day without crying and here I was bawling like an idiot over a song.

In reality it's more complicated than that. By nature I am a softie and I love to nurture just about every living thing I come across. Mothering has been one of the great delights of my life. I became who I was meant to be when my children were born. Besides caring for my kids I have filled that nurturing place in my heart by taking in foster children, teens and adults in need, a woman with a newborn baby, and endless orphaned and needy animals. I have gotten up every two hours all night long for weeks to bottle-feed baby puppies, kittens, even raccoons, squirrels and other wildlife. I'm happiest when I am babying someone. I just like to take care of everybody, to make a difference.

I can't be crying over every sad thing I encounter at work or I wouldn't be effective. Whether I am confronting an angry gang member or a cranky housewife, I need to maintain a professional demeanor. When I scoop some poor broken creature up off the road after it has been hit by a car, I don't have time to cry about it, I need to suck it up and get that animal to the emergency clinic as quickly as possible. When I'm prosecuting a cruelty case I'm all business. The tears come later, sometimes when I least expect it.

As I drove that day, tearful over the song, in a renewed surge of emotion I realized I was finally crying for Mary Jane. Mary and I met many months earlier when I was dispatched on a complaint of a dog with no shelter or water. I arrived at the address in the mean side of town and saw the dog in a rundown kennel in an overgrown front yard. She was a muscular, medium-sized black mixed breed around a year old with an eager face and a wagging tail. She hopefully watched me get out of the truck.

I knocked on the front door and a huge young man with a shaved head answered. He filled up the doorway, looking down at me with annoyance, and he answered my questions in a monotone. I asked him to walk out to the kennel with me so I could get a better look at the dog. Her name was Mary Jane. At first I was impressed that she at least had a sweet name until I remembered that Mary Jane is slang for marijuana; a fitting name for a ghetto dog.

As we approached, the dog was beside herself with joy. She wiggled and wagged and kissed my fingers through the wire, joyful for the attention. The kennel had months' worth of feces piled on one side and the food and water bowls were empty. She did have an old doghouse, however, and she looked healthy although her short coat was dirty and dull.

I asked her owner, Rueben, if she ever got out of the kennel or came in the house. He told me the dog is for protection and belongs outside. He said he doesn't let her out or she'll run away. I couldn't imagine why. I advised Rueben that his dog is required to be licensed and spayed and told him I had to cite him for both. He was obviously irritated by this news, so I optimistically played my next card. "Or you can save yourself the expense and trouble and sign her over to the shelter to find her a new home." There was a pause and I waited hopefully, but he shook his head. "No."

"I'll even waive the fees, if necessary," I added.

"No," he grumped at me.

"Then her kennel has to be scooped daily and she needs water available at all times," I said, disappointed.

"She just dumps it over," he complained.

"You're smart enough to prevent that," I said, although that could be debatable. "Try using a bucket and clipping it to the fence." I took the man's driver's license and began writing the cites and the warning for the water and sanitation issues. "You can be filling up her water bowl while I write this up," I said.

He lumbered over to the hose and filled her water bowl, then entered the kennel to get her food bowl. I was sad to see the dog went into the doghouse and laid down when the man got the hose and didn't get up to greet him when he entered the kennel. I wondered what positive training method he used to teach her to do that.

I offered some suggestions to enrich her life as I finished my cites. "Can I give you a blanket out of my truck for her doghouse?"

"No, she'll just drag it out in the rain."

To his credit there was a small soggy blanket on the ground in the kennel.

"She's bored," I said. "She needs attention, exercise, toys. What about bringing her into the house on a leash while you watch TV?" From the looks of his expansive build he watched a lot of it.

"She's a watchdog and she belongs outside to guard the house," he repeated flatly.

I had just seen this guy's driver's license and I really felt like yelling in his face, You big pussy! You are 6'3" and 330 pounds and you need a 65-pound

176

puppy to protect you? Besides, how can she protect you when you're in the house and she's out in the kennel? She probably barks at every stray cat and wandering opossum, so who would even notice if one of your gang rivals drops by to cap your big ass? She would probably lick them, anyway. But I couldn't tell him all of this because he would either kill me and bury me in the backyard for "disrespectin'" him, or complain to my supervisors and get me fired and then who would help poor Mary Jane?

I had the man sign the citations and he whined, "Can't I breed her before I spay her?" I launched into my usual passionate spiel about overpopulation and why not to breed your dog, but I could see it was lost on him. This darling dog, despite her sweet nature, was certainly not an animal that should be reproduced. Never mind that shelters are overrun with wonderful dogs and they are euthanized in huge numbers. It's infuriating that someone who has no love or concern for his dog wants to produce more of them. Does he think he would make money on her unfortunate-looking puppies?

I longed to scoop her up and drive away, but her conditions weren't serious enough to allow me to forcibly remove her. I wanted to take her home and teach her all the skills and manners she would need to be a beloved house pet. She deserved to have social interaction with people and other dogs, to have a soft bed, toys, adventures and exercise. Sadly, though, I knew that even if I required him to give her up, Rueben would probably just get another dog and put it out back where no one would see it. The key in a case like this, where it's not bad enough to prosecute, is to make it more of a hassle to have a dog than it's worth.

I couldn't stop thinking about Mary Jane. I tossed and turned that night until Paul took me in his arms and asked what was wrong. I spilled out the whole story and he held me tight and told me I can't save them all. It's a conscious effort on my part not to take on everyone's pain. It's so easy to suffer and hurt for every unloved child and animal, but it's detrimental to my wellbeing and it doesn't help anyone so I resist it as much as possible. Then again, that passion and compassion gives me the strength to do what I do. I just need balance.

I knew there are hundreds, even thousands, of dogs in similar situations all over the place that I can't help, but maybe, just maybe, I could help Mary Jane. I followed up the next week and found that the kennel still hadn't been cleaned, Reuben hadn't made a spay appointment even though we would do it for free at the shelter, and he hadn't licensed her. I again appealed to him to let us find a home for her and he refused. I wrote him another warning for sanitation, threatening legal action if he didn't comply. The conditions still weren't severe enough for me to confiscate her so I was forced to leave her again, feeling intensely frustrated at my inability to significantly improve her quality of life. All I could do was continue to check up on her and hope her uncaring owner would eventually decide to do the right thing.

Over the next several weeks I continued to drive by and check on the situation. I saw that the kennel had finally been cleaned and Mary Jane had some straw in her doghouse and some toys in the kennel. I was encouraged that her owner was at least attempting to improve on her situation. Then I found out the toys and straw were from the neighbor, Jennifer, the one who had made the original complaint. Jennifer called several times and begged me to do something. I assured her I was trying and explained that the dog's situation, while lonely and sad, was not against the law.

A month later Jennifer called me again. She wanted to offer Rueben $100 for Mary Jane. She couldn't keep her but would surrender her to us. I asked her to give me a little more time for several reasons. If possible, we didn't want him to profit from the situation. That would only encourage him to get another dog. Also, he still hadn't taken care of licensing and spaying, which gave me more leverage to work with. Last, the kennel was filthy again, so I could push the issue more if needed.

I drove to Mary Jane's home and said a little prayer that today would be the day her life would change. I grabbed my camera as I pulled in the drive. Reuben's brother, Junior, came out of the house to meet me. More personable than his sibling, Junior actually spoke rather than grunted. I started taking pictures and mentioned that Mary Jane was still not licensed or spayed. "I would hate for this to go to court," I said, snapping a photo of her empty water bowl.

The camera can be very convincing; people usually get a little more compliant when they see me getting lots of photos of the evidence. Junior said they were going to give the dog to their cousin because they couldn't afford to care for it. I cringed inside, knowing that life with the cousin could be even worse, or she could get pregnant. I shuddered at the thought of ten little Mary Janes running around and advised him that giving the dog away wouldn't get rid of the citations.

Again, I offered to take her and even to waive the fees and citations. Junior called Reuben on the phone and got the okay to sign her over. Unable to believe my luck, I grabbed a leash and reached into the kennel to slip it over Mary Jane's head. She was overcome with joy to be let out, leaping, kissing and grabbing me with her legs. More than just happy at being out of the kennel, she was ecstatic to be with someone. Some dogs are really freaked out when rescued from bad situations, afraid of the rescuer, afraid of everything. Some even try to return to the only life they knew, as bad as it was. Not Mary Jane. "Take me away, I'm yours" was her motto.

I led Mary Jane to the truck and lifted her in, quietly promising her a better life. I would shorten her name to Mary to get rid of the drug reference. I called Jennifer, who had worked so hard to improve Mary's life. We rejoiced over the phone at the dog's freedom. I had quite a few calls after that but finally got time for a lunch break at home.

My concern was that Mary would be dog or cat aggressive, which would make it unlikely we could adopt her out. The world does not need another dog fighter or cat killer. I took her out of the truck on a lead and let her loose in a small fenced yard where she could see my dogs through the fence. At the sight of my gang she started to hackle up and growl and slunk as close to me as she could. I talked happy to her and let my gentle, easygoing Doberman, Luci, into the little yard. Mary was intimidated, but she was coping, so I let the others in. They all came in and sniffed and wagged and she began to get a little more comfortable. My dogs have dealt with hundreds of fosters, so they are very smooth and have great social skills.

As Mary realized she was in no danger from my dogs and free to move around in the grass she got wildly happy and started leaping at me, mouthing, body slamming and muzzle punching, all very pushy and rude behaviors. Her assault on my body wasn't aggressive but it was certainly unpleasant. I attempted to push her off me, but she just amped up and continued to slam me. Her ripped little body felt like a punch from a linebacker and I kept turning away from her but she leapt almost face high as she continued her onslaught. It went on and on and I began to wonder what I had gotten into, but I was finally able to get her by the collar and hold her off me. Of course, she was ecstatic and overwhelmed and had no idea how to communicate with me. I held her off long enough to get her calmed down a bit and then I let go, turned away and went out into the larger fenced orchard area with all the dogs in tow. Mary had no idea how to interact with my dogs and alternately snarled at them and ignored them while following me around. I spoke softly to her and massaged her quietly when she approached without jumping all over me.

I planned to foster Mary and try to give her some manners and training to make her more adoptable. To my relief she didn't return to that extreme crazy behavior with people again, though she exhibited a variety of other obnoxious symptoms from her isolation and lack of training. She looked to me as her savior and never wanted me out of her sight. As much as I loved her already, I had to be careful to avoid encouraging separation anxiety. She needed to learn that people can be great fun but she could manage on her own for a little while.

That first day I let her outside in the larger yard with Hula for a while. Hula is a sturdy Golden Retriever who can hold her own against almost anything. I kept an eye on them through the window as Mary whined and paced and tried to force her way in through the sliding glass door every time I went through it. She chewed the windowsills and tore at the screen in her attempt to get to me.

That night I bathed her and it brought out a nice shine to her short plain

180

black coat but she was still going to be a hard sell. I brought her into the house on lead with my dogs, kids and cats. She greeted everyone like a bull in a china shop and especially liked the kids. I let her hang out on lead with the family and she was rowdy but happy. I showed her some toys and she was joyful in her play with them.

The first sign of trouble came when Mary snarled and went after Hula when Hula approached the toy. I had Mary on a leash and stopped her before any harm was done, but I could see I had my work cut out for me. Still, it wasn't unusual considering that Mary had no socializing with dogs. After a final potty break that night I put her in a crate in our room, where she could see me, and I climbed into bed. To my surprise she settled in within minutes and slept all night. It was probably the most comfortable she'd ever been.

As good as the night was, the next morning was an ordeal. I let Mary out of her crate first thing and took her collar to lead her to the door to go out with the other dogs. She didn't want to go. I had to muscle her out the door, and then she whirled around with all of her strength and tried to bulldoze over the top of me. I was half-asleep and wearing my nightgown and she was clawing my legs, forcing herself past me, fighting with everything she had in her not to go out. It was quite a battle, but in the end I managed to overpower her and got her out and the door closed. I stood there for a moment, gasping for breath, heart pounding, chest heaving and feeling lightheaded. This can't be good for me, I thought, ruefully examining the angry red scratches on my legs.

I had Mary vet checked and spayed at the shelter and put her on the website with a detailed write-up. I also took her home with me whenever possible. Most of my fosters either stay home until ready for adoption or come home every night, but Mary was so unpredictable with my dogs and cats and so strong and pushy it was an ordeal to have her at home. I have had literally hundreds of dogs fostered at my home including many large powerful breeds like pit bulls, German shepherds and Dobermans over the years but Mary was the toughest. She tore at the door frame and screens to get in if she was outside and wasn't safe with my animals unless I was right there. In the house I kept her leashed to me or on tie down where I could supervise her, but at times it was obvious she wanted to fight my dogs. I instantly rewarded any positive interaction with other dogs with small pieces of cheese or chicken.

Even though I couldn't take Mary home every night I worked with her at the shelter daily and she made rapid progress. We walked through the office to visit with the staff. She loved the attention and began to greet people calmly instead of throwing herself on them. "Sit" and "down" were mastered in a matter of minutes. She was certainly a smart girl, just very strong and forceful. She began jumping straight into her crate in the car for rides and went out like a good girl after that first difficult morning. She learned to walk nicely on a leash and wait at doors. The day she learned to play with Hula was a milestone. Full of rude energy she tended to maul rather than play. Mounting, humping, body slamming and other obnoxious behaviors abounded but at least it wasn't blatant aggression. I noticed that Hula was very tolerant and doing a fabulous job of teaching Mary what was appropriate and guiding her in a more reasonable play style. Dogs with good social skills can do wonders for the social dunces of the dog world. Jennifer emailed me every week or so for an update and I sent photos of Mary sacked out on a cushy bed in our room and playing with my dogs in the sunshine.

Mary learned quickly and every day her confidence blossomed. I continued to reward every positive interaction with other dogs and cats. She played with my dogs and other mellow dog-savvy dogs with close supervision on a daily basis, but if any toy or treat was present or if she was just in the mood, she became shockingly ferocious. As she grew more comfortable with cats she became increasingly gamey with them, less playful, more predatory. I have handled and trained hundreds of dogs and I worked hard to set her up to win. I put her in situations I knew she would do well in and praised and rewarded her with yummy treats at every positive she offered. I immediately removed her and put her away when she was aggressive; the fun stopped when she was a grouch. As she grew more confident, however, she also grew cockier with dogs, very cocky. Mary wanted to fight. She liked fighting and it was fun

182

for her. Her muscles would tense up and she could hardly wait to jump in. I could redirect her before she attacked but once she made her move she had to be physically dragged out.

From the beginning there had been a niggling in the back of my mind saying this is not a safe, adoptable dog but I wanted to make up for her terrible former life. I was personally involved and had been so thrilled to remove her from her neglectful home. I admit that I also didn't want to let Jennifer down. My judgment was clouded and I had gotten carried away by her encouragement and excitement. And I was attached to Mary. She tried so hard in every other way and loved people. To be perfectly honest, if I had evaluated her right at the start without having been involved otherwise, I wouldn't have considered her an adoptable dog.

Some dogs can get away with being aggressive to other animals. A Pekingese that wants to fight isn't super scary, more like annoying. Cat-chasing Chihuahuas are more funny than dangerous, but Mary was too powerful, too determined and too capable of causing major injury. She had also grown and filled out since I had picked her up and she weighed over seventy pounds. Of course, with a really dog savvy owner who didn't have any other pets and didn't ever want to go to the dog park and was strong as an ox, blah, blah, blah, it could work.

The trouble is that the really dog-savvy person doesn't want a dog like Mary. I probably could have kept her, managing every moment of her life to protect my other pets. I could have continued to make improvements, kenneled her when I wasn't watching her and most likely have kept everyone safe. But one slip up, one miscalculation, one gate not firmly latched could mean disaster. I was not willing to risk my pets or anyone else's.

And yet still I stalled from the inevitable. I had turned dog-aggressive dogs around before. One beautiful German shepherd named Reba had attacked every dog in sight when I took her in. She was completely at a loss about how to interact with dogs and was intimidated by them so her response was to attack in an attempt to drive them away. Within a month of training and confidence building she could safely go to the dog park and became a wonderful companion to a friend of mine until her death at ten years of age.

But Mary was different. The more time she spent around dogs the more she wanted to fight. It was just her personality. I continued to take her out daily, to train and exercise her and work on her dog issues. Some days she seemed better. She often played with another employee's mellow neutered Golden Retriever, Rusty, and I was able to reward that behavior, plus she enjoyed playing with him so that was its own reward. I still kept the lead on her for safety but left it slack as they played.

Finally the day came when everything came to a head. Mary was playing with Rusty as I chatted with his owner, Karen. Suddenly, Mary snarled horribly and launched at Rusty's throat. She got a mouthful of his ruff in her teeth and shook her head violently. Rusty tried to cower away as I yanked Mary back. She stood on her hind legs, lunging and snarling, her entire body bulging with aggression and tension, and a mouthful of Rusty's hair was stuck in her teeth. I called her name and dragged her away, attempting to redirect her, but she focused her blazing eyes on Rusty with one goal in mind: a fight to the death. In her excitement she whipped around and bit my arm, ripping my jacket before turning her attention to Rusty again. Thankfully, her teeth hadn't penetrated my skin. I dragged her around the corner and out of his sight while she continued to struggle to get at him. It was several minutes before she calmed down enough to respond to me. I asked her to sit and she did, so I gave her a treat and she wagged her tail and smiled at me like wasn't that fun? Karen had put Rusty in her office and she came out to where I was and gave me a meaningful look. "What are you doing?" she asked.

"I know, I know," I said, fighting back tears. "But I love her. And part of the problem is the neighbor worked so hard to help this dog and I'm afraid she's going to freak out and hate us."

"We have a responsibility to keep other animals and people safe. There are too many nice dogs that need homes," Karen said. "Why don't you send the neighbor an email and let her know what's going on and see how she responds."

If Mary had been a high-profile case like the Michael Vick dogs (a pro football player convicted of dog fighting) we probably could have gotten her into a reputable rescue but she was just another one of the thousands of poorly bred, neglected and poorly socialized dogs in the world. In the big picture there are too many dogs and not enough homes. Too many friendly, happy dogs that don't want to kill other dogs go without homes.

I put Mary back in her kennel and went about work that day with a deep ache in my soul for what had to be done. Finally at the end of the day I sent an email to Jennifer letting her know that despite months of work, Mary was too aggressive with other animals to be considered a safe dog to adopt out. I thanked her profusely for her help and concern and waited with dread for her reply.

After a sad and sleepless night I went to work the next morning and checked my email. To my amazement Jennifer was kind and gracious in her response. She admitted she had once rescued a dog that she had worked with for a long time and finally had to euthanize it due to similar issues. I was practically in tears with gratefulness that she understood. Our job can be so difficult and often people on the outside don't understand and judge and vilify us for what we have to do. I was called Hitler by a few extremist former volunteers when I was doing much of the euthanasia at the shelter years before, one of the saddest, hardest jobs an animal lover can have. Someone once said that euthanasia should be done by people who don't like animals and I vehemently disagree. The last thing any animal should know is the gentle touch and soft voice of a caring person. Thankfully, our shelter has an excellent adoption rate and I wasn't euthanizing friendly, healthy animals, mostly animals with serious health or temperament problems.

I could have asked the technicians to euthanize Mary without me but I have a policy to be with any animal that I am attached to for euthanasia, both to comfort them and for my own closure. I took Mary out on the shelter lawn for a long time and played with her in the morning sun. She ran joyfully through the grass, tossing a stuffed toy in the air and coming to me for a massage every few minutes. Her tail wagged and she smiled up at me with her big pink tongue

185

lolling out. She was still plain, but she had filled out and her coat had a nice sheen to it. She had experienced some of the fun things in life. Finally, I leashed her up and went to find one of the shelter technicians who is a dear friend. She is a compassionate and loving person with a special affinity for dogs. We took Mary to a private room and sat down on a blanket with her. I cuddled her and rubbed her tummy and told her she was a terrific girl and I loved her and she leaned against me in delight. The technician gently inserted the needle and Mary slipped away in my arms, knowing nothing between bliss and eternity.

I was numb for a while after that. I have had to euthanize other animals I was attached to before, my own beloved elderly pets and fosters I had spent a lot of time with. Still, it really takes it out of me. I had tried so hard for Mary. I put so much of time, energy and emotion into improving her life. I did my best to focus on the fact that she got to enjoy life for a little while, that she got to run in the grass and be loved, that she slept in a cushy bed, played in the sunshine, had tummy rubs, and didn't produce any unwanted puppies.

Almost every week I get happy cards and emails from adopters of my former fosters. Animals I was able to rescue, save, nurse back to health and find homes for, hundreds of animals in whose lives I have made a difference. But it still hurts that I couldn't save Mary. And until that song came on the radio, I hadn't even been able to cry. I pulled the truck over for a few minutes and sobbed hard. Finally, I blew my nose and pulled back onto the road.

31. Casual Friday

A pointy black nose with a white stripe down the middle was just visible behind an ice chest on the patio. I slowly stepped closer until I could see the little black button eyes peering calmly at me. Skunks, as a rule, aren't worried about much. Confident in the abilities of their potent arsenal, besides the occasional spritzing of a wayward dog, they tend to amble around, minding their business.

I find skunks attractive and the babies are as playful as kittens. I have fostered and rehabbed litters of them for wildlife rescue. This one was supposed to be sick: the caller had said it was acting strangely, out in the daytime and not leaving the area in the presence of people. Nocturnal wildlife out in the daytime is not always a sign of illness, although it can be. There had been some outbreaks of distemper among the local skunks, and I was dreading having to shoot another sick skunk; there's no cure for distemper. Skunks not only always release their scent when dispatched, but I hate killing them even when it's an act of mercy.

As I looked closer at this little creature I saw no sign of illness, in fact, she appeared the picture of fat, shiny good health. She studied me curiously with only an occasional warning lift of the tail if I moved suddenly. Looking around the patio I saw that it was completely enclosed by a high wall and the only access other than through the house was a long, steep flight of stairs up to the road above. The home was a beautiful beach house, built into the side of a hillside overlooking the ocean. I wondered if the skunk was just having trouble ascending the stairs. Down would be easy, but up might be a trial, and skunks are among the most unathletic of creatures.

The caller, Mr. Hanson, was a kind-faced older gentleman, on a weekend getaway with his wife to celebrate their wedding anniversary. He peeked around the corner at me. He seemed to think the animal had fire hose type capabilities and was reluctant to be on the same planet with her, although he was concerned for her welfare. When I advised him I thought she might be stuck rather than sick, he looked relieved. "What are you going to do?"

What indeed?

"Well," I ventured, "I'm hoping to annoy her just enough to leave, but not enough to spray."

The secret to successful skunk handling is to move extremely slowly. An inch at a time, I pulled the ice chest away from her, removing her hiding place. The tail rose threateningly but she didn't spray. I backed away from her and began making a racket, banging a stick against the wall and yelling. She put up with it for a while and then begrudgingly toddled toward the stairs. She looked up the long, steep flight of steps as if it were Kilimanjaro and scrunched herself into the corner against the bottom step.

It was time to up the ante. I grabbed a nearby hose with a spray nozzle and turned it on, spraying water in her direction without dousing her. She averted her head and tried to scoot away from it, but I swished it back and forth in front of her until she turned again toward the stairs.

It was time to begin the valiant climb to freedom. The skunk placed her little front feet on the first step and struggled mightily to get the rest of her rotund body onto it. She could get a back leg up but her fat little belly seemed to hang her up. I wondered if she was pregnant, though it was a little late in the season for that. She looked over her shoulder at me a few times to see if I was going to let her off the hook as she worked. At last, she heaved her belly up and over the step and sat panting slightly. Hoping to keep up the momentum I continued to squirt the hose in her direction and, after an eternity, she managed two more steps. It was taking her about five minutes per step and she still had over twenty to go.

The ascent ended on step three. Fifteen minutes in, the skunk had stalled completely, and no amount of yelling, banging the stick or spraying with the hose would move her. She even stopped threatening to spray, she just lay down on the step and watched me.

Now what? I was running out of options, which called for desperate measures. Holding my breath, I flattened myself against the far side of the stairway and squeezed cautiously past her and up the stairs to my truck. I grabbed a thick blanket out of the truck and then worked my way back down the stairs and got below her again. Holding the blanket out in front of me like a shield, I advanced. I lowered the blanket onto the skunk while attempting to hold the offending tail down and scoop her up in the blanket. How round and fat she was, like a cantaloupe in a skunk suit. To my surprise, she didn't struggle or try to bite, and I carried her quickly up the stairs to freedom. The neighbors, who had been following the saga at a safe distance, cheered as I reached the top with my charge snuggled like a baby in her blanket.

I set the skunk down in some nearby bushes, satisfied I'd gotten away with it, when I suddenly caught a wave of powerful odor drifting up the stairway. I looked down the stairs, and there it was: the odious small yellow puddle of skunk spray pooled on the third step from the bottom. She had obviously sprayed straight down as I lifted her. I hadn't taken a direct hit but I was definitely in the stink zone. I staggered back, fanning my face and searching for a fresh breath of air. Meanwhile, my odiferous friend waddled off in the direction of a nearby creek, probably headed for some much needed sleep. I dropped the blanket in a nearby garbage can and said waved good-bye to a rather stunned looking Mr. Hanson.

Even without the rank-smelling blanket, the odor in my truck was overwhelming, and I headed home for a change of clothes. In the garage I took off my boots and pants and dropped the pants into the washer. There didn't seem to be any smell to my shirt. Clad in only my uniform shirt and panties, I went in to change. Our housemate, Mickey, sat in a chair reading. When I said hello she looked up in her characteristically unruffled manner and took in the sight of my bare legs and lacy panties for a moment before asking "Casual Friday?"

32. Mudslides, Electric Lines and Rottweilers

The rain pounded my windshield as I squinted to see in the darkness at 2:00 a.m. Blue and red lights flashed up ahead as I steered the truck closer, peering through my wipers as they whipped back and forth. Emergency vehicles were everywhere and rainwater streamed across the pavement as a police officer flagged my truck around a barrier that closed off the road. I could see a half dozen firefighters illuminated in the bright lights from the trucks, the rain slanting across them. A dog was stuck in a mudslide somewhere around here.

I parked out of the way and approached the nearest firefighter. I couldn't hear him over the pelting rain, but he gestured for me to follow him. In my flashlight beam I caught sight of a home partially buried in mud, with twisted trees and other debris poking up here and there. I couldn't see much of the rest of the hillside in the dark, but it loomed over us and didn't seem very stable. This would be a get in and get out as fast as possible situation. Dispatch had told me someone had already been removed from the home with serious injuries.

As we struggled through the mud to the back of the house all I could see was an ocean of brown goo. I couldn't imagine how anything could be alive in there. Several of the fire crew worked back there and one of them pointed a light at some downed power lines across part of the yard. "Stay away from those!" he hollered over the din. The crew stopped what they were doing and one shone his flashlight and pointed into the gloom. A tree had come down with the hillside and it lay sideways in a mass chaos of limbs.

It was hard to see in the blackness ahead of me, but I thought I saw a slight movement. I walked toward it, trying to ignore the mud sucking at my boots and oozing over the tops of them. It was the dog.

Crouched miserably, eyes squinted against the rain, the dog was half buried in mud. He glared at me as I approached, and a deep growl rumbled loud enough to be heard over the rain. Even covered in mud and half buried, I recognized the broad head of a Rottweiler.

Well, this is nice, I thought: pouring rain, mud to the knees, unstable hillside, downed power lines and a grouchy dog to top it off. Not that I could blame the poor guy. "Hi, buddy," I called over the roar of the pounding rain. "You're going to be okay." Cautiously, I slipped a lead over his head. I was ready to jerk my hand back if needed but I could see he couldn't go very far even if he wanted to. The mud came halfway up his rib cage.

I attempted to pull the dog free while a firefighter held the light. A few others tried to help me pull the dog loose, but he wasn't budging. The men got their shovels and began digging around him as I tugged the lead and encouraged him while trying to keep my footing in the mud. It felt like pulling a mountain. And then it dawned on me. The dog was chained to an object buried deep in the mud. Carefully, I reached under his massive jaws to unclip him. In the dark it was hard to gauge his reaction to me messing around his head, but fortunately he didn't eat my face. As soon as I released him he surged forward and we were able to pull him out. When he realized he was free, he followed me gratefully.

By the time I lifted the filthy dog into my truck and poured a pint of dirty water out of my boots I was covered in mud from head to toe. I put a clean towel on the seat before climbing in and headed through the storm to the shelter.

In our warm intake room I toweled the dog off and looked him over for injuries. He seemed okay, so I settled him on a blanket in a kennel and headed home to bed.

The next morning's paper stated that the dog's owner, sixty-two-year-old Myrtle Brown, had been pulled from the house with a broken leg and other injuries. The article said she was grateful to be alive but sad because her beloved dog Tank had apparently perished in the slide. I had mixed feelings about that. How beloved could Tank be when he was chained outside all night in a storm? Still, he was her dog and she at least needed to know what happened to him.

I called the hospital and was patched through to a nephew who was there visiting. He told me the dog had been abandoned at Myrtle's home by a grandson who had left town some time before. Tank was too rowdy for Myrtle to handle as she was in poor health even before the accident. But she sat outside in a chair with him every day, bought him the choicest kibble on her limited income, and put a cushy bed inside his doghouse. She even had a dog-loving neighbor who walked him a few times a week. Well, that was better than a lot of dogs get, but now Myrtle had no home at all. Tank was around eight years old and although he was sweet with people when he wasn't buried in mud, he wasn't good with cats or other dogs, so adopting him out would be difficult.

We kept Tank at the shelter for several weeks while Myrtle healed and searched for a place to live. She was ecstatic that Tank had survived and kept saying she wanted him back, but it's hard to find pet-friendly housing and even harder to find places that accept big dogs.

Tank settled in and was a good boy and we all grew attached to him. Each time I passed his kennel he wiggled his butt in delight and shoved his huge head against the wire for a scratch.

I was getting worried we were running out of options, but on a Saturday morning a shaggy-haired young man came striding into the shelter and declared he was Myrtle's nephew and he was there for Tank. He said Myrtle had found a rental with someone who had seen a follow-up article on Myrtle and Tank. The landlord lived next door to the rental and loved Rottweilers. He even offered to help train Tank and hoped to integrate him into the house with Myrtle, where he could be a house companion. The place even had a dog door to a fenced yard so Myrtle wouldn't have to walk him.

I went out to the kennel to get Tank and thumped his broad rib cage as he wiggled against me in delight. "You be a good boy," I said, as I handed him over to Myrtle's nephew. I wiped a tear from my eye and went back to work.

33. An Old, Old Dog

The job always seems to know when I desperately need sleep. I had an injured deer that morning at 4:00 a.m., too early for a full night's sleep and too late to go back to bed. I then worked a ten-hour shift, came home, fed the kids, fed the animals, helped Shay with her homework, went to sleep at 11:00, and now it was 11:30 and my phone was ringing.

The caller urgently described a horribly abused dog wandering in the streets near his home. I needed to respond immediately, he said, with lights and sirens if possible. When asked how he knew it was abused he explained that it was emaciated and could hardly walk. Now, the word "emaciated" doesn't get me too excited because most people use it to mean they can see a little rib. From his description, it sounded more like an elderly, arthritic dog than one in dire straits, especially if it was well enough to be "wandering."

I told the caller we didn't have the staff to attend to strays after hours and asked if he could confine the dog overnight until we could pick it up in the morning. The shocked gentleman informed me that he was a member of the Humane Society and that this poor animal was suffering and likely wouldn't survive until morning. It needed immediate veterinary attention and I must come before it expired in the street. I had grave doubts, but I told him I was on my way. "Hurry!" he demanded. "It may die before you get here."

Twenty minutes later my headlights picked up the figure of a skinny old yellow Lab standing in the street. A clean-cut and well-dressed middle-aged man waited on the curb near her. One glance at the dog told me she was ancient. The white muzzle, fleshless skull, and milky eyes spoke of tremendous age. She was a little arthritic and thin, but I could also see that this was a beloved pet that had wandered away. It was not an abandoned animal. She was immaculately clean, her coat had the silky texture of a house dog, and the nails were neatly trimmed. To top it off she had a pink collar with tags. "Have you tried to call the number on the tags?" I asked.

"Of course not!" he snapped. "I would never return a dog in this condition to the owner. They must have dumped her!"

He seemed certain this dog was horribly abused and abandoned while I was just as certain that she was not. "She's very elderly," I said, "but she looks well cared for. And why would someone abandon a dog with tags?"

"How can you say that?! She's skin and bones and they probably just forgot to take off her tags. Besides, how do you know she's old?"

After many years it's as easy for me to spot an old dog as it would be to identify an old person, outside of Hollywood that is. I tried to point out the signs of age to him, but I could see he had didn't believe me.

Tired of standing in the street arguing in the middle of the night, I slipped a lead on the old dog, copied down the number on her tag and went to lift her into the truck. Old and a little disoriented, she snapped at me as I picked her up. "Oh no, old girl, you're okay, you can't bite me," I said, as I avoided her nubby old teeth and placed her gently in on a thick blanket in the dog box.

"She wouldn't bite you!"

The man was outraged that I would say such a thing about this sweet animal. I tried to explain that she was old, scared and arthritic and it would be perfectly normal for her to try to bite a stranger, but I could see he thought I knew nothing about animals. He was sure I was afraid of this poor, abused dog.

The man was insistent that I rush the dog to the vet and press charges at whoever did this to this poor creature, throw the book at them. Prison was too good for them. If I wasn't going to do anything about it he would go to the newspapers, the five o'clock news, the mayor, anything to bring justice. I studied the man's face in the light from the streetlamp. "Sir," I said, "I will take the dog to the vet. Here's my card. You can call and check up on her tomorrow."

I drove around the corner, then dialed the phone number on the dog's tag. It answered on the first ring. "Oh, thank God!" gasped the frantic woman when I told her I had her dog. "I took her out to go potty in the front yard and got distracted for a moment. When I looked for her she was gone."

"Hey, listen. The finder was a little worried about your dog. Can you meet me at the emergency vet clinic in a few minutes?"

"Of course," she said. "Sadie is eighteen years old and was at the vet a month ago for a checkup, but if you think she needs it I'll be right there."

Jeez, I thought, eighteen? She looks fabulous for her age. "I think she's fine, ma'am, but we just want a quick vet check to make sure."

Ten minutes later the vet gave her a quick exam and declared her in amazing health for her age. As I passed her off to her tearful owner I realized that the man who called was probably worrying himself sick. Certain he would still be up fretting about my incompetence, I gave him a quick phone call with the good news that Sadie was healthy and reunited with her loving owner. There was a long pause. "What about her being so skinny?"

"Many of these really old animals just don't process their food well anymore but she still has a good quality of life."

He asked a few more questions and thanked me for calling, but as we hung up I realized he was unconvinced. He just knew the vet and I were wrong.

34. In The Barn

I groaned aloud as I read my list of calls for the day. I had to meet with the infamous Edgar Dinger regarding yet another complaint about his animals. My coworkers all started teasing me. "Oh, Shirley, you know Edgar will be thrilled to see you!" joked Rich, rocking back in his chair and laughing uproariously. Jim called out, "Hey, Shirley, I think you're just his type. And I know he wants to go on a ride-along with an officer." I glared at him, but I knew it was all in fun.

I'd never met Edgar, but his reputation preceded him since our department had been to his house many times before. Tales of his lack of hygiene and the fact that he was always looking for a date were among the main topics of discussion when someone returned from Edgar's house.

Edgar was said to be a bachelor in his late forties. The trouble was that he had two neighbors who were afraid of him but called us frequently about his animals. It wasn't that we didn't believe the callers, it was that we had been unable to prove any violation of the law. They called because Edgar's black Labrador had puppies under the porch. It's certainly nicer in the house, but the

198

pups were fine and it's not against the law. They called because he butchered a hog in his backyard. They called to report that his sheep weren't sheared, called to tell us his chickens were scruffy. We had never been able to get Edgar for anything other than a cite for dog licenses, which he had kept current since then.

I had driven by Edgar's rundown place numerous times but this was the first time I turned into the driveway. The complaint was that animals were locked in a barn without food and others were unhealthy, so I surveyed the place with a critical eye. It was raining and there was an assortment of livestock in his bare, muddy front pasture — sheep, goats, turkeys, chickens, geese. They wandered among old tires, machine parts and other junk, but I could see an open shed they had access to and they looked healthy enough.

I parked and approached the weathered front door. There was no overhang and rain dripped on my head as I waited, but finally the door opened to reveal a large, balding overweight man with a scruffy beard. He wore a bathrobe that wasn't nearly long enough and he greeted me warmly, showing a lot of crooked yellow teeth.

As I started to introduce myself he interrupted and invited me in. I declined but he insisted. "Come in, come in, I'm not going to stand here and get wet." Of course, I know better and I always try to avoid going into people's houses. If the animal issue is inside there is no way around it, but I really didn't want to go inside with this guy. Still, the rain was blowing through his front door so it was a reasonable request. And our officers had been dealing with Edgar for years; he could be obnoxious but he wasn't threatening.

I stepped into the dimly lit kitchen to the odor of bacon grease, unwashed bodies and wet dogs. Two black Labs and a big hairy brown mutt crowded around, sniffing and wagging. They were dirty and needed brushing but looked healthy and happy enough.

The inside of the house was as shabby as the outside. Edgar ambled into the living room and flopped down on a ratty couch. His robe climbed his thighs alarmingly as he put his feet up on the coffee table and patted the seat beside him. "Come sit down and tell me what the trouble is."

"Oh, thanks, but I sit too much in the truck as it is," I said, averting my gaze and keeping my distance. "I'm Shirley from Animal Control and we have been asked to check on the welfare of your animals. Can I take a look at them?"

"What's the problem now? You people were just out here."

"There's some concern about the health of your animals, but I assure you I will take as little of your time as possible. If there's no violation, the call will be closed as unfounded."

"I want to know who's making these complaints." He narrowed his eyes and picked his teeth with a thumbnail as he glared at me.

"Well, how about I go and take a look and I'll let you know if there's any problem." I was trying to make a hasty retreat without looking as unnerved as I felt. "No need for you to get wet."

"No, you're not gonna walk around my property by yourself," he said.

"Then come along and let's get this over with," I said, edging toward the door.

He heaved to his feet, grumbling about the weather. I almost shot out the door and waited in the rain while he threw a raincoat and hat over his bathrobe and joined me. He showed me different shoddily fenced areas containing pigs, goats and sheep. Large numbers of poultry wandered the property, but none of the animals really looked unhealthy. I asked him to show me where all the food was kept and how much he fed. I hadn't yet seen anything that was a violation but wanted to make sure I wasn't missing anything in the various closed barns. "Do you have any other animals on the property?" I asked, over the drum of rain on the tin roofs.

He beckoned toward one of the barns. "Over here." He graciously opened the door for me and I stepped in out of the rain. He came in behind me and shut the door and switched on the light. I looked around the room with growing unease. It seemed we were in a storage area stacked high with old dusty machinery, ancient furniture and boxes. The walls were covered with pornography and there wasn't an animal in sight. "Can I offer you something to eat?" Edgar asked, reaching into a dusty fridge and holding out a yogurt as pink-nippled Miss November stared seductively from a poster on the cobwebbed wall behind him. His body blocked the door and the robe and raincoat gaped dangerously almost all the way up his leg. I tried to respond lightly but firmly. "No, thank you. I don't see any animals in here so I'd better get on my way."

Edgar continued to block the door and he reached back in the fridge and held out a root beer. "How about a drink then? You should really try this."

"No, thank you. I have other calls to attend to and I need to be going." I was fighting panic by then, wondering how long it would be before dispatch checked on me. I toyed with trying to force my way past him but he was at least six inches taller and a hundred pounds heavier than me. I could smell his musky body odor and see the pouty gazes from the provocative posters of impossibly big-busted nude women all around as I tried to stay calm. We had a standoff at that point, with him blocking the door and reaching toward me with the soda, and me, probably looking like a deer in the headlights, refusing it. There was a moment of silence while he stared at me, his gaze unreadable. The hair on the back of my neck prickled. He seemed insistent that I take something so I finally took the soda, hoping to appease him.

"Well, thanks for the drink. I don't see any problems here, so I'll just close the call." I moved purposely toward the door, hoping to get him to move through sheer force of will. It didn't work.

"How about some salami?" he offered. I had the major creeping willies by then and could feel my heart pounding so hard it seemed he would see it beating through my chest. It was obvious he was stalling. I could try a quick call for help on my hip radio, but help was far away and I didn't want to escalate the situation.

I tried again. "I better get going or dispatch will send a search party after me," My tone was joking, but I hoped to remind him that people knew where I was. He seemed to snap out of it at that point and opened the door.

I was tearful with relief as I headed for my truck where Luci whined anxiously from the cab. She sniffed me all over as I turned the key in the ignition and it was obvious she was picking up on some of my distress as she licked my face and almost climbed into my lap. I gently pushed her back and restrained the urge to gun it out of the driveway. I headed to a park across town, pulled in and cut the engine. I sat there for a while, taking deep breaths, stroking Luci's silky head and trying not to think about what could have happened. Maybe he was just trying to be friendly, but I tend to be somewhat naive. I force myself to read the newspaper every day just to remember that not everybody's nice. I turned on the radio, attempting to distract myself from horrifying visions of rape, murder and sex slaves locked away for years in barns like that one. I'll take dangerous animals any day. It's the people that scare me to death.

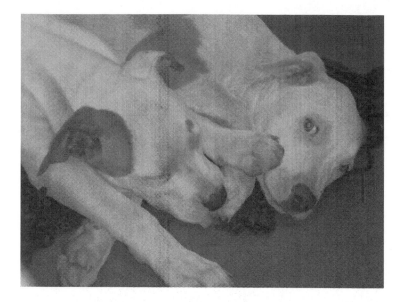

35. The Cadillac

The incessant ring of my cell phone penetrated my dreams until I realized what it was and rolled over to glance at the clock: 11:30 p.m. After spending my evening wrangling loose cows off the highway I had only been asleep for twenty minutes.

I grabbed the phone. Maybe I could talk someone through whatever it was and go back to sleep. But the voice of the police dispatcher quickly dashed my hopes. A police officer made an arrest and needed two dogs removed from a vehicle immediately. I dressed quickly and headed out the door.

The officer waited for me on a busy downtown street next to a parked Cadillac. In the glow from nearby neon signs I saw two girls standing by the vehicle and a clean-cut, sharply dressed man seated in the back of the patrol car. A diamond the size of a golf ball glittered in his ear. The girls looked like they were in their teens and were hardly dressed for a cold night. I was wearing a uniform, heavy boots and a warm coat and I was still a little chilly. They wore very short skirts, high heels and tight, low-cut tops, and they shivered as they waited.

I was still half asleep but slowly my brain began to process what I was seeing. I looked closer at the girls and felt a pain in my chest. In their haggard young faces I saw a couple of girls who really needed to be loved and helped. They didn't seem to be under arrest. I doubted they were even eighteen. I overheard one of them tell the officer they came over from Oakland, a city about an hour away. I may be naive but it boggled my mind that people drive to other counties to sell little girls on the street, like it's a business transaction or something. I was overwhelmed with sadness.

I tried to bring my mind back to the job at hand and glanced into the caddy. I didn't see any animals. The officer directed me to the trunk. "The dogs are in back," he said, rolling his eyes. I pulled two slip leads out of my pocket and cracked the trunk slowly, unsure of what I might find. My flashlight beam landed on two wiggly young pit bulls straining to lick me as I slipped leads over their heads. One fawn and one brindle, they appeared to be littermates of maybe eight months old.

Once I got the leads on I opened the trunk all the way to remove the pups. I was surprised at the size of that trunk: in a pinch they could conduct business back there. The pups were ecstatic to be free and they leapt around at the end of the leashes trying to kiss me, the officer, and the two girls as I led them to my truck. The girls bent over to give the dogs a quick pat and the officer averted his eyes in alarm as the skirts revealed way too much.

After loading the pups onto a blanket in the back of my truck I took the slip of paper the officer gave me with the owner's information and said goodnight. Glancing at the paper I was not surprised to see that the dog's names were Felony and Cujo, typical bad-ass pit bull names. I looked back at the girls once more, standing silent on the dark sidewalk. I wished I could take them with me, too, help them, show them another way of life. My stomach churned as I drove away.

At the shelter I vaccinated, wormed, impounded and fed the pups. By the time I headed home it was 1:30 in the morning. Paul was away on a work trip and I couldn't sleep. Those girls weren't much older than Nikki, who slept

204

peacefully in her cozy bed in her flannel pajamas. Nikki's biggest worry this evening was whether she'd get an A on her Spanish test the next day.

Over the following weeks, as required by law, we sent letters to the dogs' owner, but he never responded. I hoped he was in jail and would never get out. And I checked on the pups daily. They were kenneled together and always greeted me ecstatically with wagging tails and attempting to lick me through the chain link. Maybe riding around every night in the pimp mobile was good socialization because they seemed confident and adaptable and had delightful temperaments.

We changed their names to Allie and Charlie and they passed their health and temperament evaluations with flying colors. They were spayed and neutered and offered up for adoption. It took a while, but finally Allie went home with a terrific firefighter whose last dog had recently died of cancer. Charlie was adopted by a family with teenaged kids and a big yard.

Looking back I can see the similarities between the girls and the dogs. All were adolescents at the mercy of a man with his own interests in mind. At least Allie and Charlie were living a wonderful life now. I still wonder about the girls and hope they have a better life now too.

36. I'm So Insulted

I dreaded my daily visit to check on Harry Hiener's horses. His was one of those in-between cases, not bad enough to forcibly remove the horses but serious enough that we had to monitor their care and feeding each day until conditions improved. Sometimes, I had been lucky and he wasn't home. Then I could quickly view the horses, document the amount of feed in the ramshackle barn and be on my way.

A round, balding, argumentative man of around fifty, Mr. Hiener didn't appreciate my intrusion due to the simple fact that he knows everything there is to know about horses. That I think several of the horses in his care were seriously underweight and the others didn't look that great was simply lack of knowledge on my part.

During the original call several weeks earlier, I found nine horses in varying states of health. A couple of them looked okay, several more were thin enough to be cause for concern, and two mares were in bad shape. Most of the horses were Thoroughbreds, racehorses, who tend to be lean, but this was ridiculous. The property, too, didn't look like any racehorse facility I had seen before. I thought of the immaculate ranches I had seen, with sleek, beautiful horses grazing in pastures of lush grass, and graceful barns without a fly in sight.

This place was a total dump. I can sympathize with lack of money for fancy barns but there was no excuse for this. Empty feed sacks and garbage littered weed-infested paddocks, piles of wire and debris lay among the weeds, causing a safety hazard for the delicate and high-strung animals. The fences were falling down and the wooden sheds that provided meager shelter for the horses were eaten clear through in spots by bored and hungry horses. I stroked their silky noses and hoped that what I was doing would make a difference.

Mr. Hiener had finally agreed to sign over the skinniest horse, a mare named Candy, to a rescue group, but he insisted she had been getting four flakes of alfalfa and six pounds of grain daily and just wouldn't gain weight. Candy had seen a vet a few months before, he said, and had been skinny when he got her, but I was unable to verify this.

I know some horses are truly difficult to put weight on, so I was trying to give Mr. Hiener the benefit of the doubt and work with him. My mother had gone through it. She had once bought a skinny mare with the idea of fattening her up. She had her vet checked, floated her teeth, wormed her and started her on the best of hay and supplements. But the mare flatly refused all grain and supplements, ate hay when it suited her and didn't gain an ounce. More pricey visits from the vet and years of excellent care followed but made little difference. She remained on the ribby side for the rest of her long and otherwise healthy life.

Candy disproved the possibility of just being a hard keeper. She immediately gained at least fifty pounds with a few weeks of good care in a foster home.

Almost worse than Mr. Hiener were his two daughters. Dishwater blondes somewhere in their late twenties and still living at home, they were riddled with bad skin and bad attitudes. They hated me on sight and followed me around griping and disagreeing with everything I asked them to do. If they were home and their father was away, they usually called him immediately and spent the entire time on the phone whining to him about my unreasonable requests. Statements from me like, "This horse is completely out of water" or "Your horse has a bunch of wire tangled in its tail," were considered highly offensive.

In all but the most severe cases we have to spend a lot of time trying to educate animal owners and give them the opportunity to improve the animal's care. Sometimes that's all that is needed to improve a situation and people thank us for the help. The added bonus to taking the time is that if things don't improve and it does end up going to court, the judge can see we have made every attempt to assist the owner. At that point the animal can usually be confiscated and removed from the owner for good.

Some people are very willing to work with us on their animal issues, but Mr. Hiener wasn't one of them. On this particular day he came grumping out of his house, intent on arguing with me before I had even said a word.

"Why are you here again? I told you my horses are fine."

"Sir, your horses are too thin."

"They are not too thin. I would starve myself before I starve my horses!"

Mr. Hiener was standing on his porch, somewhat above me, and my vantage point at the bottom of the stairs put his ample gut just about at eye level. The hairy white expanse flopped in a massive roll beneath his soiled white T-shirt and over his belt. I was having trouble processing his remark about starving himself when facing the evidence of his obvious gluttony at close range. Momentarily stumped by the absurdity of his statement, I finally managed to respond.

"Your horses are seriously underweight, Mr. Hiener," I stated firmly.

"That's your opinion," he shot back.

"No, sir, it's the vet's opinion," I said, trying to keep my voice steady.

Dr. Miller had seen the horse that was surrendered and was appalled by her condition. Harry looked me up and down and then replied with a sneer, "Well, I think you're too skinny. That's my opinion."

And I'm thinking, Wow, way to go, loser. You really know how to insult a woman. Mr. Hiener didn't know I had already filed charges with the district attorney's office, but he would be finding out soon enough.

That evening after work, I spent time with my own pampered horses. After many, many hours of patient handling, Annie was a different animal. She grew more accustomed to the saddle and I began to have her wear it while I lunged her and worked in the round pen. Next I introduced the bridle and she accepted it without much trouble, so each day when I worked with her I tacked her up fully. I led her around the property and down our quiet lane. She seemed to enjoy these outings. I started leading her while I rode one of the geldings. She was pretty leery of having me anywhere above her and I hoped this would help acclimate her. Sometimes I put her in the round pen and pulled her head around a bit, tying the reins to the saddle. I would sit on the fence and supervise as she learned to give her head to the pressure. The beauty of this is that the timing is perfect. The second she gives her head, the pressure is released. She bumps against the bit, circles, bends her head, learning all the time. After twenty minutes or so, I release her, have her trot a few easy circles around me, and then I tie her head the other direction and resume my position on the fence. Shay comes out and climbs up there with me and we visit until the sun dips behind the hills. We take Annie into the barn and un-tack her, and then Shay helps me feed the horses. That night I ate a double serving of dessert.

Within a few months, Candy looked stunning. She had gained several hundred pounds, her coat glistened and showed good health, and she was adopted into a wonderful home. The courts gave Mr. Hiener a slap on the wrist, but I occasionally drive by his place and his horses do look better. Who knows, maybe he learned something from the experience. Like how to keep irritating little blond ACO's off his back.

37. The Nose

Sometimes the complaints we get make me laugh. A small red and white dog wanders over to the nearby grammar school every day and makes off with the kids' lunches. This morning he took a lunchbox, ran for home with it and a child had to chase him down the school driveway. The dog turned out to be a Basenji mix named Sebastian.

I could picture it so clearly. Little Sebastian cruising onto the school grounds each day looking for a snack. He was a well-cared-for little dog, but he apparently enjoyed his own foraging to eating his same boring kibble. The kids left their backpacks leaning against the wall outside of the classrooms each morning and Sebastian would sniff from bag to bag. Hmmmm…peanut butter and jelly, apple, bagel. Ahhhh, turkey sandwich, now we're talking. Sebastian would grab the whole Scooby Doo lunch box and head for home. But, whoops! The offended owner of said lunch box sees him through the classroom window and sprints out the door and after the culprit. The thief looks back. Uh oh! His little curled tail unwinds and streams out behind him as he rockets for home, but it's awkward trying to carry a lunch box and run too. The boy is gaining on him, and Sebastian, sensing trouble, drops his loot and doesn't stop running until he reaches his home.

And that's where I found him, relaxing innocently on his front doorstep. His owner was a mellow-looking woman with flowing brown hair and an equally flowing blouse and skirt. She was surprised to see me and she looked at Sebastian lying quietly on the doormat. "I'm sure there's been some mistake," she insisted. "He never leaves the property." I assured her it was indeed her little choir boy, verified that his license was current and gave her a verbal warning.

I drove away, still grinning at the whole scenario but refocused quickly when dispatch gave me a call of a dog attack with injuries. I copied down the information and whipped a U-turn to head to the address. As I drove I called the victim to find out what happened. Bob Maloney explained that he was attacked and bitten on his own property by his neighbor's two American Bulldogs. He wanted to meet with me, so I drove first to his house.

As I pulled up Mr. Maloney came out of his house and waved to me eagerly. He was middle-aged and heavyset, with thinning brown hair. I was glad to see he didn't appear to be seriously injured. There was a small Band-Aid across his nose, but there were no other signs of an attack by two 100-pound-plus dogs.

He pointed out the high chain link fence that separated his property from the dog owners' property. As we looked at it, I noticed a strong odor in the air, not exactly unpleasant but I couldn't place it. I forgot about the smell as Mr. Maloney proceeded to explain that he had been leaning close to the fence to making a repair in it and his nose had accidentally gone through the wire. He was bitten by one of the dogs, he wasn't sure which one, from its own side of the fence.

I looked at the fence in confusion, trying to figure out how he could have managed to "accidentally" get his nose through. He did have kind of a big nose but it still didn't make sense, and besides, if his nose was on the other side, wasn't it trespassing? As I was still trying to understand the logistics of the whole thing, I heard ferocious snarling and barking coming from the back of the yard next door. A pair of enormous American Bulldogs roared around the corner and hurled themselves at the fence. They bayed and snarled at us with fearsome intensity and specks of saliva flew from their mouths and hit me as I quickly stepped back. White with brindle markings, they stood on their hind legs against the fence to give us a closer view of snarling mouths and big white teeth.

Most of this breed that I've dealt with have been friendly, but American Bulldogs have been bred as protectors and guard dogs and this pair clearly took the job seriously. Shaken, I handed Mr. Maloney a complaint form to fill out and asked him to send it in. I then headed next door, thankful for the sturdy fence that kept the dogs from entering the front yard. Nobody in their right mind would approach within ten feet of that fence with those killers raging and slavering on the other side of it, let alone put their nose against the wire.

Again, there came the strange smell, and I sniffed the air in puzzlement. It seemed vaguely familiar. Several large billboard-style signs stood in the yard and I glanced at them as I walked toward the front door. One read: BOB MALONEY, LEAVE OUR NEIGHBORHOOD AND TAKE YOUR POT WITH YOU. The other said: THE WEED IS NEXT DOOR, DO NOT ENTER THIS YARD. A large red arrow pointed to Mr. Maloney's house. I sniffed the air again. Of course! I had been part of enough drug busts to realize it was marijuana I smelled coming from his backyard.

The dog owners were an attractive young couple in their thirties with a spotless, beautiful home. They invited me in. Upon hearing the accusation against their dogs, they glanced at each other in exasperation. The man spoke first.

"We saved for years to buy this house and didn't realize until after we moved in that our neighbor has a medical marijuana license. That wouldn't be a problem except that all kinds of riffraff keep coming by to either buy or steal it."

The woman ran her fingers anxiously through her hair and continued the story. "We bought Rex and Clark because people were either knocking on our door wanting to buy pot or climbing over our fence and going through our backyard in the middle of the night trying to steal it from his yard. We have been trying to get him to move his garden to a more rural location instead of here in town, and he's not happy with us."

The law requires that we quarantine the animal when there is a report of a bite, so even though I had serious doubts about the whole thing, I asked that they keep the dogs confined on the property for ten days just to be sure and I waived the usual quarantine fee. They were nice about it and I finished getting their information and handled a few more calls before heading back to the shelter.

When I arrived, my supervisor handed me a stack of photos and said that someone named Bob Maloney had dropped them off for me. I was eager to see the photos. The first was a startling close up of his face with the nose almost filling the photo. I squinted closely at it but could not see the slightest hint of an abrasion. If he was trying to prove that he was not bitten it would have been more effective. There were several more photos of his unmarked nose and then more of the fence and the billboards on his neighbor's lawn. I don't know what interest he thought I might have in his neighbor's signs; it was completely irrelevant to the "bite" or any other animal issue. So many of our calls are really for people issues, neighbor disputes and that type of thing.

I had to leave work early that day to take Luci to the vet and I quickly forgot about Mr. Maloney and his maimed nose. Luci had been off her food, and for a dog that had gained five pounds in four days when I left her with a friend who free-feeds, this was serious. The only other time she missed a meal I rushed her to the vet to find out she had pneumonia. I'm not much of a worrier, but she's just so precious to me. I stroked her silky ears as I drove to the vet.

I used to work for my vet and the clinic was still like home to me. I chatted with the staff as I waited, and I greeted Dr. Patti with a warm hug. In the exam room Dr. Patti checked Luci over, we discussed her symptoms and she took some blood and sent us on our way. I'd get a call with the test results when they came in.

Luci leaned her head across the seat of the truck and rested it on my lap as I drove home. Besides missing a meal or two, she seemed fine. Maybe it wasn't anything serious. At home that evening, she ran and played in the field with the other dogs as I worked with Annie. Later, Paul said she ate most of her dinner, and I felt a little better. The kids were bickering and Shay needed help with her homework, so I was busy for the rest of the evening and when Paul and I finally fell into a deep sleep.

38. The Cliff

Being called out of a deep sleep and away from a sweet, warm husband at midnight is a highly overrated pastime. Being called out at midnight when it's freezing cold and raining is in a class by itself, especially when it's clear across the county and I can't find the address and have no cell service to get hold of the caller for better directions. The caller had said that she and a friend were staying at a guest house on the coast and they had rescued a stray dog that had been hit by a car. She told me the dog was bleeding and they had her in the house with them wrapped in a blanket.

An injured dog is certainly an emergency and I ran through the rain to my truck. It took forty-five minutes to reach the small seaside town where the call was located, and when I got there I missed the turnoff in the dark. After consulting my map book and turning around I found my way to the narrow lane. It was nearly impossible to see any addresses in the pouring rain and I crept along, rotating my overhead spotlight in an attempt to read the address numbers. Wind buffeted the truck as I wound higher and higher up the hillside. The lane was barely wider than the truck and frightfully steep as it hugged the cliff. It

215

must have a gorgeous view of the ocean in daylight but tonight it was like a black hole.

At last the road leveled out somewhat, but as I rounded a corner I came to a dead-end at a locked gate. The address on the gate wasn't the one I was looking for and there was nowhere else to go and no room to turn around. I had come to the proverbial end of the road. It was after 1:00 a.m., I had no cell service and backing down in the pitch black was unthinkable.

I shone my spotlight to the left. As I suspected, it was a sheer cliff. I couldn't see the bottom and there was a steep hillside rising to my right. I pulled my hood over my head, got out with my flashlight, and peered closely at the road as the water poured over it and rain lashed my clothes. The pavement was truly only a foot or so wider than the truck. I walked about fifty yards back down the hill until I found a place that was slightly wider. I stomped around at the edge of it to make sure I wouldn't sink down and shuddered at the sight of the cliff. It was a long way down.

In the truck again, I kept the driver's door open and the flashlight propped so I could see as I cautiously backed down to the wider area. I tried not to think about what would happen if I miscalculated as I began what I later jokingly called a forty-point turn. Moving forward and backward by mere inches, I rotated the truck. There was one terrifying moment when the tires slipped on the mud at cliffside and I lost traction. Frantically, I turned the wheels as much as I dared and they finally caught and held and I continued inching around until I faced downward and was able to take my first deep breath. It was another twenty minutes of inching along and driving up unmarked driveways before I finally found the correct address.

The two friends on a vacation getaway were thrilled to see me after the long wait and they ushered me inside. Rainwater dripped all over the rug as they showed me the dog. I was relieved to see she appeared to be okay. An attractive fawn and white pit bull, she whipped her tail at me and tried to lick my hands as I examined her. To my surprise, she appeared in perfect health. "Where is she injured?" I asked.

216

"Look at her back foot." One of the girls pointed.

Picking up the offending limb I stared at a slightly bloodied toenail. "Is that what you mean?" I asked. I was beginning to process that I had driven in the rain for half the night and nearly fallen off a cliff to an early death for a torn toenail.

"It was really bleeding before," the other girl offered.

"I thought you said she was hit by a car."

"Well, when we saw it was bleeding we thought that might have been what happened because we found her in the road," the first girl said with a shrug.

I stared at her for a moment and decided the damage was already done. They were genuinely concerned about the dog and hadn't intended for me to nearly plunge off a cliff. I took a deep breath, thanked them for their help, and the dog and I headed back into the storm.

39. Bad News

The next morning at work, I downed multiple cups of coffee as I sat at the computer. Luci hadn't touched her breakfast and I was getting really worried as I glanced at her snoozing on her bed under my desk. I was still half-asleep from my late night at the coast and was having trouble concentrating on my work. My cell phone rang and I found Dr. Patti on the line.

"Shirley," she said, quietly. "Luci's lab work doesn't look so good."

My heart froze in my throat. "What's going on?" I managed to ask.

"It looks there's a problem with her kidneys," she said. "Can you bring her into the clinic right away?"

I knew this was not a good thing.

Bless my darling and flexible supervisors who allowed me to take the rest of the day off. Twenty minutes later Luci and I sat in the exam room waiting for Dr. Patti. Luci laid her head in my lap and I stroked her face while a million thoughts jumbled my mind. Not my Luci. My darling Luci, my dear friend and protector. I always felt so safe with her around. On days that no adults were around when the kids got back from school, Luci stayed home to be there for them when they walked in the door. I knew she would never let a stranger in without permission.

Dr. Patti finally came in and she gave me a long hug. "It looks like she's in early kidney failure. Her kidneys are pretty bad, but there are things we can do to help. I want to start her on IV fluids and some medications right away to try to kick-start her kidneys into working better. Can you leave her here for the day?"

I sat in stunned silence. Two days ago she had seemed perfectly healthy. And I knew kidney failure is pretty much a death sentence. The trouble with kidney failure is that dogs don't usually show symptoms until it's too late. I was having trouble processing that I was likely to lose her fairly soon. Finally, I took a deep breath. "So what kind of time are we talking?"

"It's really hard to say. It depends on how well she responds to treatment. Maybe a few weeks to a few months. Some of them do really well and go longer."

I drove home in shock. It was so strange not to have Luci in the seat beside me. At home, the other dogs crowded around, sniffing my clothes for a report of my doings. Paul had left to fly overseas for work and the house was quiet. I sat down on the couch and stroked the dogs, lost in thought.

40. A Short First Ride

I lay flat on my back in the round pen. It had all happened so fast I wasn't even sure how I got there. Luci whined and fussed from the other side of the fence. Thankfully, she was starting to feel better on her kidney medications and was back to being my shadow. Paul was bending over me and Annie stood on the far side of the pen looking bug-eyed.

I slowly rose to my feet, checking for injuries. Other than some bruises and abrasions, I found none. I walked over to Annie, stroked her muzzle and cuddled her sweet face to my chest. "What's the matter, honey?" I asked her. She sighed and leaned into me as if to say, "That was really scary."

After many months of saddling, lunging, driving, and tying tires, gunnysacks, feed bags and all the rest to the saddle and letting her carry them, we'd had our first ride today. A very short ride. I had climbed on with no trouble and had sat quietly astride for a moment to let her get used to my presence there. At the first step, she panicked at the strangeness and unfamiliarity of me on top of her and bolted around the pen. Her MO when she's scared was to run, so I figured I would just let her run. The round pen is small and she can't go anywhere, anyway. Unfortunately, however, being unaccustomed to the added weight on her back, she stumbled and went down hard, throwing me into the fence before leaping to her feet and tearing off in a wild gallop. As always, once the perceived threat was over, she calmed and stood quietly again. There was no malice in her actions, just a need to protect herself from something terrifying and new.

The first ride I'd taken on other horses I had trained had been a total nonissue. They hadn't been the least bit bothered by my presence on their backs. But Annie had a history of wildness behind her and the fact that she tamed at all was rather miraculous. I had spent far more time training her for this first ride than I had with the other horses, but she clearly wasn't ready to be ridden. I hadn't done my groundwork thoroughly enough for a wild horse. I climbed on again and sat for a moment but didn't ask her to move. Back to the drawing board.

With Luci sick, I hadn't been able to work with Annie as much but she still had come so far in so many ways. Once Luci stabilized, I began training Annie more again. Her first bath was a piece of cake. One sunny morning I worked her for a while. She had become quite accustomed to both the saddle and bridle, and I lunged her daily wearing both. Once she had worked up a sweat, I led her around the neighborhood from the back of my gentle gelding, Joe. Being focused on the new scenery was a good way for her to get used to new things and not worry about the tack. Back at home, she was relaxed and calm. I removed the saddle and bridle and turned the hose on low. Starting at her feet I gently ran the water up and over her body. She wiggled away a few times but really did well. I sudsed her from head to toe with a big sponge and then rinsed her. She made less of a fuss than Roanie does during a bath and Roanie has been handled since birth. Annie had filled out and she positively shone in the sunlight. Her thick black mane and tail rippled with highlights. I stood back and admired her. What an improvement from the skinny, scruffy, matted animal she had been.

I had also taught Annie to drive. No, this doesn't involve getting her

221

behind the wheel of a Chevy. It means running a couple of long lines from the bridle to the rear of the horse. You then walk behind and teach the horse to turn and give their head to the bridle as well as to stop and back up by pressure on the bit. The lines spooked her at first, but, like most things, she got used to them after a while. Soon, from behind her, I had her doing figure eights, halt, back up, and walk and trot.

I didn't have a horse trailer then but I really wanted to teach her to load, so I started taking her into tightly confined spaces, up and down concrete steps, and into my shop and sheds. I let her take her time, rewarded her, fed her inside and then let her out. I also worked on her getting used to every possible thing she could come across on a trail. Natural obstacles like creeks and hills were no trouble at all as she had encountered them on the range.

I wanted Annie to be comfortable with all kinds of manmade objects as well. I hung tarps, buckets and plastic bags around her pen and touched her with them while I worked her. I even laid a tarp on the ground and wasn't concerned with how long it might take. I just wanted her to walk across it. I led her up to the tarp; she sniffed it carefully and then walked across like it was no big deal. I was so impressed. We were really building a level of trust.

But she still wasn't completely comfortable with me above her. I spent a lot of time ponying her (leading from another horse) with my geldings to get her used to having me higher than her, but she wasn't crazy about it. I could see now I had been way too hasty in climbing on her when I did.

I continued working with Annie every chance I got, but sometimes work and the fosters kept me so busy weeks passed with no more handling other than grooming her a few times. Paul is helpful, but he's not really horse savvy and I don't have a great setup for training, so when my friend Tim from the DA's office offered to let me keep her at his place, I jumped at the chance. He offered to pick Annie up and take her to his house, where he has a great set-up for horses, including a round pen and a huge sand arena. I told him she had never trailered before other than being shot into one from a livestock chute at the BLM but I thought I could get her to load.

222

When Tim pulled up with his rig, I led Annie to it and let her check it out. Fortunately, it's a spacious three-horse slant, which is more open than a straight-load trailer. I stepped inside while Annie sniffed around. The step up into the trailer was about 18 inches high and there was no ramp.

"Let's go, Annie," I said, giving a confident tug on the lead. She stepped up with her front feet, felt the slight give in the trailer and backed out. I got out, walked her in a circle and led her straight to the trailer without hesitation. She jumped in behind me and Tim closed the door. Yes! I was beyond thrilled. She had loaded into a strange trailer on the second try, with no fuss.

At Tim's, Annie settled in right away. He lived only three miles from me and I stopped by after work when I had time and often spent a few hours there on my days off. Over the next few months I worked on acclimating her to every possible thing we could. We ponied her from the other horses, sat on the fence above her, and continued to drive her until she was sensitive to the slightest touch of the bit.

I was concerned about riding Annie in an open space because of her panic and her previous fall with me on her. She had also spun away from me so quickly several other times when I was handling her that she had lost her footing and fallen down. She didn't seem klutzy, but she could be so reactive she sometimes outran herself. In most ways she was gentle, but I had to stay alert.

One day, I was leading Annie to Tim's round pen and she was walking quietly by my side. Suddenly, she whirled around, ripped the lead out of my hands and galloped off toward a wooded area at the back of Tim's property. What was that about, I wondered, glancing at my raw hands. I had forgotten my gloves and gotten another rope burn before giving it up and letting go. The *chop-chop* of a helicopter overhead must have been the culprit. Then I remembered that wild mustangs are often rounded up by helicopter. I went to her and she allowed me to catch her, but she was shaky and jumpy and we didn't go anywhere for a while. Poor doll, I crooned to her, stroking her mane. Nobody's going to hurt you. You're okay. She finally released a shuddering breath and followed me back to the barn.

Anne remained very hesitant to have me above her. Tim and I decided we had to get her used to me working somewhere she couldn't get away from me. We started closing her into a narrow chute where she couldn't go anywhere and I spent a lot of time on the rails there above her. I rubbed her coat, scratched her neck and put weight into the saddle. It's very dangerous to be in such an enclosed area with an unpredictable animal, but I always made sure that Paul or Tim were there and I was ready to move away from her quickly if she freaked out. If I fell underneath her where she couldn't get away I could be stomped to death.

When the time came, I started sitting on her for about thirty minutes at a time and she gradually quit worrying about me being up there. Next, I climbed on and off her in a roomy stall with Tim holding her lead. Again, this can be extremely unsafe if I came off and she couldn't get away from me. But I felt that as well as I knew her it was the best way to progress. I was right. Now I could move her in small circles in the stall. I could move her out, walk her in both directions and stop and back her in the stall. She seemed to be adapting to my presence on her back, even while moving.

On a Sunday morning I drove to Tim's with butterflies in my stomach. It's funny to me that when I was a kid I climbed on every horse I came across, trained or not, and rode off without a second thought. If they bucked or ran it just added to the fun, but now I had to admit I was nervous. I don't feel as indestructible as I did in my teens. I have a husband, kids, and a mortgage, and none of them need me in a full body cast. Also, Annie was a very different creature from the uber-domesticated horses I had dealt with when I was younger. Annie had learned a lot in her time with me, but I had learned more about horses from her than any other horse I had ever worked with.

I tacked her up and worked her in the round pen until she was completely calm and relaxed and then led her around until Tim got home. I wanted someone there to call the ambulance if needed.

It was the moment of truth. We took Annie into one of the small paddocks and Tim held her while I climbed on. I sat on her quietly for a few minutes, stroking her neck, and then asked her to walk. Would she freak out like before or would she deal with it?

Annie moved out like a dream, walking along the fence line until I asked her to whoa and gave the barest touch on the reins. She stopped and I stroked and praised her for a moment before asking her to walk again. As she calmly circled the pen at an easy walk, I had an intense feeling of accomplishment. I felt so close to my little girl who started out so scared but gave me a chance. We did some gentle turns and circles and a couple more stops before I climbed off. I wanted to end on a good note. After un-tacking her, I spent a few moments grooming Annie, scratching her itchy spots and telling her what a good girl she was. The awe I felt was overwhelming. This animal had been through so much. She had come to trust me, had carried me on her back and even seemed to enjoy my company. We had shared a tremendous learning experience and developed a deep bond. When I released her into her pen, she stayed beside me until I left and then watched me walk away.

41. A Pig's Tale

A call came in about a limping goat on a property visible from a busy
road. The stock owner wasn't home, but his young son showed me the animals.
The goat had a minor deformity to the leg, which caused a little hitch to its gait.
It didn't seem to be in pain, was in good overall condition and there was food,
water and shelter available. I checked on the rest of the animals on the property
to make sure their conditions were acceptable.

The place was pretty run down with sheep, goats and poultry
wandering among rotting boards, wire and other debris. The animals appeared
healthy, though, and I was preparing to leave when I heard the sound of a pig
squealing. I began trying to locate the animal. I traced the sound to a pile of
produce boxes and other garbage. I could see a large plastic bin about four feet
square and three feet high, the kind you see filled with grapes during harvest in
this wine grape–growing region. It sat haphazardly among the junk, tilted
slightly as if it were just thrown there. It was covered with a pallet with a piece
of plywood across the top.

I peered inside. The pig was there, trying desperately to shove her nose up through a gap in the boards. Flies and yellow jackets buzzed as I moved the board aside a bit and looked in. It was a young Duroc, one of my favorite breeds, with a bristly red coat, and she could only move a couple of steps in any direction. The box was filthy and the floor rotted into a cesspool underneath. There was no food or water. I grabbed a hose and filled her tipped bucket. To my surprise, she wasn't thirsty. She had probably been watered that morning and then tipped her bucket over in the tiny space. She was more interested in playing in the water and interacting with me. She looked quite healthy, bright-eyed with good weight and coat.

Pigs are highly social, intelligent and playful animals and this one's conditions were unsanitary and unacceptable. I tried calling her owner on his cell phone but he didn't answer. I pointed the box out to the young son and told him the pig couldn't live there. She needed to be moved into a suitable pen or she would be confiscated. If there had been any other place to move her I would have done it myself. I gave him my card and asked him to have his father call me immediately. I hated to leave the pig, but because she appeared healthy I had to give the owner a chance to rectify the situation. I took photos of the conditions and put in some straw to give her a dry place to lie down.

Driving away, I wished I could take her with me and give her a wonderful life. I felt a little subdued that evening. I prepared Luci's special food and cuddled her, but I kept thinking of the pig, unable to even see another animal, walk around or enjoy the sunshine and dig in the dirt.

The next day I returned and met with the pig owner, who took me out to see what he had done. I was delighted to see the pig had been moved to a spacious pen, with access to sun and shelter. It was still a haphazard thing, made of pallets with plywood over the top, but she had a tub of sparkling clean water, fresh food and plenty of room to move around. There were sheep and goats on the other side of the fence to socialize with and a fat duck waddled through her pen. Not as good as another pig, but some companions nonetheless. There was also a cool dirt floor to root around in, satisfying her need for physical and mental enrichment.

The pig was busy with a major excavation project at that moment, with her front legs in her hole and piles of dirt around her. She looked up at me with a little mound of dirt still balanced on top of her rubbery nose and *umph-umphed* at me with satisfaction. As I watched, she flopped down in her hole and sighed contentedly. Such a little thing, but it warmed my heart. The pig's owner wasn't a monster, just uneducated in the basic needs of animals and the law. He was willing to work with me, and the quality of life for a needy creature was greatly improved because of it. In the scheme of things this wasn't a big deal, but for one little pig it made a world of difference.

42. Tyra

A tall, lanky black dog huddled in the corner of the kennel. The kennel card said, "Stray Lab Mix," but closer inspection showed her to be a scrawny adolescent Great Dane or Dane mix. Apparently, she had been found running scared in a supermarket parking lot.

When I went in with her, the dog flattened herself against the wall and refused to come near me. I tried sweet talk and cookies without response, and when I attempted to slip a lead over her head she dodged it in terror and snapped at me. Her panic when I looped her told me she had no idea what a leash was. Instead of traumatizing her further in the noisy kennel, I scooped up all sixty-two pounds of her and carried her out of the noisy building.

Out on the shelter lawn, I couldn't get much out of her and a peek at her teeth showed her to be a baby of only about six or seven months old. She didn't seem much like a puppy with her size and attitude. Anne said she had been working with the dog for a few days, while I had been off, just sitting in the kennel with her and hoping to get her over her fear of people. The puppy appeared to have had no socialization whatsoever. She didn't have the faintest idea how to cope with anything new, a common response for dogs without exposure to the world in those critical first months. She had probably sat in someone's backyard for her entire short life and was understandably traumatized by her new and noisy environment.

She sat through her stray waiting period and no one claimed her. I wondered about her history. Had someone bought her and then decided a puppy was too much work? Or had a litter been bred by someone with dollar signs in their eyes who had then found no market for the pups? Regardless of her past, no one was going to adopt a big terrified dog with no training that was scared enough to potentially bite someone. Especially when that dog was going to be as big as a donkey when she finished growing.

With my darling Luci in renal failure and a mom and litter of pups at home already I certainly didn't need another foster, but I've always liked Danes and something in the hopelessness of this pup's demeanor spoke to me. I decided to take her home and work with her.

Other than the first few times when she snapped at me, the dog was almost completely unresponsive. It was as if she knew there was no joy to be found in life, it was just something to be endured. Fairly quickly, she stopped trying to bite and figured out the leash. Within a day or so she followed me miserably wherever I went, but she showed no interest in me or her surroundings. I brought her into the office while I worked on a lengthy report. She curled up on the bed I provided next to me and failed to move unless I made her. She refused every treat I offered and didn't seem to enjoy the stroking and massages that I and others at work gave her. She did perk up and offered a slight tail wag when she saw Anne, the first person to have connected with her, but that was it.

The first night I brought her home she greeted Nikki and Shay with a hesitant tail wag and a kiss, which was more than I had gotten out of her. Then she curled up on the nearest dog bed in the living room and stayed there the entire night. When my kids were little they had a Veggies Tales tape and one of the songs on it was called, "The Pirates Who Don't Do Anything." This became her theme song, and I sang it to her often as she lay there. She may as well have been a stuffed dog for all I could get out of her. No interest in me, my dogs, my cats, people, even toys. Warm fresh chicken, canned food, liver treats, you name it, all were spurned. She did eat the bowl of kibble I offered, but that was it; she refused to take anything by hand.

After the first few days I realized she wasn't terribly fearful anymore, just depressed and traumatized. I took her to work each day as I didn't want to leave her unattended at home. Once, I took her to the fenced shelter yard to go potty and made the mistake of letting her off leash. Unleashed, she refused to have anything to do with me. I finally had to get Anne, and between the two of us we got her cornered and leashed again. She spent another catatonic day lying in her bed beside me at work and offering no interest in the world. That night, except for another mild greeting she made to the girls, she did the same at home. Most dogs want to bond with me within a day or two, but not this girl.

My family hashed over some names for her but couldn't settle on one. Finally, one night Nikki and Shay were watching a show starring model Tyra Banks. Mickey overheard the show from the kitchen and said, "The dog's black, she's pretty and she has long legs. Her name should be Tyra." And Tyra it was.

One evening, Paul was cooking his special meatballs for Luci and I offered Tyra one without much hope she'd take it. To my surprise she ate it eagerly, so I started offering small bits of them every time I approached her. I noticed she had started coughing occasionally and suspected she was coming down with kennel cough. Though we always vaccinate for it at the shelter, dogs sometimes get it anyway. It's common in shelters and other places with a lot of dogs and, like the common cold in humans, it's quite contagious. It isn't usually helped by antibiotics, but because of the stress the animals are under and their proximity in the shelter, we often start medications for secondary infection. It's not much of an issue for dogs that are healthy and unstressed, so I wasn't too worried about my dogs at home, except for Luci, whose health was already

231

compromised. I consulted the shelter vet and started Tyra on antibiotics. Dogs usually throw off kennel cough in a few days.

On antibiotics, Tyra's cough was controlled, but she stopped eating entirely. She'd sniff at the tidbit in my hand and stretch her neck out slowly and gulp but refuse the treat. It was obvious her throat hurt, so I tried warm homemade chicken broth but she refused that as well. She was still drinking a little water but I started to worry when she refused food two days in a row. I had plenty of subcutaneous fluids at home for Luci, so I injected 500 mls under the skin hoping it would help combat dehydration. She was thin to begin with, and now she was so skinny and weak I worried she would get pneumonia and die. I coaxed her with everything I could think of without luck. Then one morning she woke up hungry and ate her breakfast and made up for lost time.

A lot of traumatized dogs are much more afraid of men than women, but Tyra was more comfortable with Paul and some of the guys at work than she was with some of the women. She warmed up to Paul before she did me and began greeting him like a friend. Over the following weeks I took her to work daily and had everyone give her treats and let her approach at her own speed. The day she hopped into the car on her own was encouraging, and soon she started greeting us with a prance in her step and a wagging tail. I handed treats to everyone who was willing to give them to her if she approached them and she started getting more comfortable with people.

Tyra's coat had been dull when she came in but I started noticing some patchy spots and took her to the vet. Yuck: demodectic mange. This type of mite is usually present in the skin of healthy dogs in small number but in dogs with poor immune systems or other trauma it can proliferate to the point of serious problems. She would need months of expensive toxic dips and oral medications. I dutifully started treatment. Poor girl, what else did she need to suffer from?

Tyra wasn't housetrained and I'm normally so strict about supervision that I never allow any accidents in the house, but I was distracted giving Luci her fluids one day and forgot to keep an eye on Tyra. I walked into the living room to find not only a lake of urine but a mountain of poop. I had never seen such volume. I guess there's a reason not everyone has giant dogs. Feeding a big dog like that each day was also an experience. I have owned several very large dogs, including a male Borzoi that was well over 100 pounds. But none of the others ate anywhere near the amount Tyra ate. Her appetite had returned and she was filling out and expanding daily. I could almost see her gaining weight. As she grew the classic beauty of the Dane showed through in every way.

The more I could improve Tyra's behavior and health, the more likely it was I could find a good home for her, so I started working on teaching her to play and to respond to "sit" and "down." She learned quickly and her confidence improved as she learned what was expected of her. For fun we started working on tricks. She learned "Give me five," "other five," "speak" and "take a bow" in rapid succession. She seemed to really thrive on the training, waiting eagerly for the next request.

Because of Luci's illness I didn't spend as much time with Tyra as I would have liked, but I continued to take her to work with me each day and I rewarded every positive interaction. I advised people to ignore her and let her approach them, and she grew happier by the day.

Soon, her tail was wagging every waking moment. She became such a happy girl it became a problem. While she's mostly very gentle, her tail is a serious weapon. I had welts on my legs a few times from getting smacked by it. Her height is a problem, too. Once poor Paul got the tail-smack right in the crotch, leaving him doubled over in pain as I hovered over him anxiously. Thankfully, he recovered his health after a period of convalescence with me doting on him.

43.A Second Chance

If only I could have a few hours of uninterrupted time this morning. I could finish my report and get it submitted to the District Attorney's office by this afternoon. I was working on a cruelty case and had done a thorough investigation complete with witness statements, photos and a veterinarian's report. Now I just needed another hour or so to put on the finishing touches and I would be done.

Of course, a call came in. A German shepherd was chasing sheep on

Meadowlark Lane. A dog in livestock is a serious situation and Meadowlark is at the far reaches of our jurisdiction, nearly an hour away. Chances were either the sheep would already be dead or the dog would be long gone by the time I got there, but I had to try. My report would have to wait.

It was a sparkling, sunny day and I enjoyed the drive in spite of my anxiety to get there as soon as possible. Nearly an hour later, I turned onto Meadowlark Lane. Almost immediately I saw a group of sheep huddled in a corner of a pasture and staring nervously in the distance. I couldn't see a dog but the sheep were obviously frightened and I could hear a dog barking beyond some trees at the far end of the pasture.

I pulled over and got out but couldn't see a gate or any sign telling me who owned the sheep or whose pasture it was. Since we can't trespass on private property unless it's a life or death matter, I was considering what to do. Suddenly, I heard frantic bleating coming from the same area as the barking and my decision was made. In seconds I scaled the fence, snagging my pants on the barbed wire and grimacing as I heard a long rip. I began the long trek across the field and, what do you know, there, on the other side of a bank of trees, was a German shepherd chasing sheep.

I knew he had been at it for over an hour by now, and he was visibly tired but having way too much fun to stop. The shepherd's tongue hung halfway to his knees as he loped after the terrified sheep. He reminded me of the old coyote and Roadrunner cartoons where both are so worn out they walk with tongues dragging though the coyote is in hot pursuit.

I hollered at the dog and he stopped in surprise, still far from me. At first his posture was so stiff as he stared at me I thought he might charge me. I tried calling and sweet talk, but he stood his ground warily, so I continued to trudge across the field in his direction. I kept talking as I approached, and he began to look fearful. It seemed he would bolt and be gone at any moment. To my surprise, however, he remained in place, and the closer I got the lower he got. I used my gentlest, most upbeat voice but he sunk down almost imperceptibly until he was completely lying down and then he rolled over and wet himself as I reached for him. This was just a big pup, probably less than a year old, a nice-looking German shepherd with the classic black and tan markings.

When he was leashed, had his ears scratched and realized I wouldn't hurt him, he got up and followed as I looked for victims. Sadly, I found a dead lamb in the pasture. The lamb didn't have any visible wounds; it just appeared to have been run to death. Sheep cannot tolerate prolonged physical exertion and often collapse and die from stress when chased for long periods. None of the other sheep appeared injured and I was thankful I had slipped my camera in my pocket and wouldn't have to hike back for it as I photographed the dead lamb and the dog. "You are so busted, young man," I sighed.

As we began the long walk back to my truck I worried about the dog. Our job as officers means that we have to protect animals, including livestock, and people's livelihoods as well. This dog was young, friendly and attractive, but shelters don't usually want to adopt out livestock killers, so unless he was claimed by an owner willing to take full responsibility for his actions or taken by a rescue, he could be euthanized. It's such a shame because it's a normal predatory behavior. Most dogs will harass or kill livestock if given the opportunity. It's the owner's responsibility to train, confine and manage their dogs to keep them safe and prevent problems.

I couldn't lift the large dog over the fence where I had climbed in as it was five feet high and topped with barbed wire, so we had to go a long way around the fence line to find a gate and then load him into my truck. My next task was to try to locate the owner of the dog and the sheep. I asked at a nearby fruit stand and was directed to a house farther down the road.

As I pulled in the driveway I could see a ramshackle doghouse in a small rundown pen with shoddy fencing that backed to one side of the field where I had just been. A sweet-faced young Spanish-speaking woman answered the door. In my very limited Spanish I was able to confirm that it was her dog

"Oso" and that he was always kept in the pen, but today he had escaped. I called a Spanish-speaking supervisor to explain the situation more clearly to her. The woman could keep the dog if she had a safe place to confine it, was willing to go to court, pay restitution for the lamb, and accept citations for dog-at-large and licensing. If she chose to sign the dog over to the shelter and pay for the lamb we would waive the citations and court. It was easy to see this was an outdoor dog with no training and not a lot of attention, so I was relieved when she chose the latter option.

Dealing with the sheep was the next piece of business. The sheep belonged to the dog owner's landlord. I called him and found him very supportive of his tenant and understanding about the lamb. He did not want the dog euthanized. He was truly a reasonable gentleman in every way and I assured him I would do my best to get the dog into German shepherd rescue.

I thought about the dog on the way back to the shelter. He was young, strong and healthy and obviously had a lot of drive. He seemed to want to do what I asked and was probably highly trainable. I contacted a local police dog trainer who had gotten dogs from our shelter before and he came to evaluate Oso. After spending time with him at the shelter and a trip to the vet for x-rays to check his hips, the man took Oso home to train for a law enforcement career.

Today, the dog, renamed Trigger, spends his days riding around in a patrol car with his proud handler, sniffing out drugs and busting bad guys. Days off are spent at home with the family and nights sleeping in the bedroom next to his handler's young sons. Trigger has come a long way from his crummy little isolated pen and his days of chasing sheep.

44. How Do You Say Good-Bye?

As our time together grows shorter, I find myself battling thoughts of the unfairness of life. My precious Luci, my protector, my gentle friend and doggie soul mate, will be leaving me soon. Her kidney failure is irreversible and terminal. She takes endless medications and I give her subcutaneous fluids daily to buy her some time and keep her comfortable, but no amount of protest, medical care or railing against the inevitable will change what's coming.

Having always owned multiple pets I've faced this many times before, but somehow with Luci it's different. She's younger for one thing, and although as a child, many of my pets were killed suddenly by cars, as an adult all of my animals have lived to be elderly. As much as I love kissy, waggy puppies, it's the old dogs that get to me, the faithful friends with graying muzzles and patient demeanors that have been there through thick and thin.

Luci would be eight soon, much too young to be dying. Until recently,

238

she'd been the picture of beautiful shining good health. An adolescent stray when first found, she had a total lack of manners but a wildly exuberant good nature. No one claimed her during her stray holding period at the shelter and when Paul learned that I had fallen in love with her, he gave her to me as a gift for our thirteenth wedding anniversary.

Luci had been found in good condition but was missing the last inch or so of her left ear. We jokingly called it an ear cropping gone wrong. She had been allowed to keep her small, beautiful ears and I loved the way they fold back neatly alongside her head instead of hanging hound like next to her face like many natural-eared Dobes. She also had a pellet of some sort under her skin where she had been shot at some point, most likely for chasing livestock. There had been a report of a black dog chasing sheep in the area the day she was picked up.

I often wonder what became of Luci's original owners. Had they bought an eight-week-old Doberman with high hopes and been overwhelmed by the normal antics of a puppy? Peeing, pooping, chewing, whining, barking, and chasing the neighbor's sheep? I imagine they meant well. Luci was healthy, friendly and well fed but she wasn't house-trained, didn't know any words and was pretty out of control initially. I could see some poor person being bowled over by her exuberance and tired of trying to housebreak a puppy in winter.

Regardless of Luci's history she quickly won over the hearts of everyone who met her. With time, exercise and training she settled into the perfect companion. Absolutely loving, totally reliable in the house (at four years of age I still can't leave Hula unattended for five minutes inside and she doesn't get into something), gets along with every animal and person I bring home. Luci doesn't try to eat my free-ranging chickens like Katie the Borzoi does and yet is sensibly protective. She is an amazing ambassador for Dobermans. One woman who visited fell in love with Luci and was happily stroking her sweet face. When I said something about her Doberman traits the woman immediately jumped back. She wasn't afraid until she heard Luci was a Doberman.

Luci sleeps a lot more now, snug in her big cushy bed and covered with a soft blanket. I often sit with her, giving her the massages and tummy rubs she loves. When any of us pass by we inevitably stop to give her a kiss and a cuddle. She lies awake and watches me for long periods while I read or work at the computer. It's almost unnerving, those beautiful dark eyes piercing my soul and looking into my heart. I often stop what I'm doing and go to her then. In the past she would have gotten up and come and leaned against me with her head in my lap. I finally realized that when she stares at me, she wants to be with me but feels too ill to come over, so I go to her. I lie close to her and stroke her sweet face until she falls asleep and then I listen to her rhythmic breathing until I'm forced to try to get something done and leave her until she wakes again.

When the sun comes out she'll ask to go out and spend an hour or so lying the sunshine where it reflects off the little puppy barn in the yard. I watch her from the kitchen window while I clean up, thankful she came into my life.

Luci's protectiveness has been a factor in our being able to cope with Paul's long work trips of up to several weeks at a time. As sweet and gentle as she is, she also recognizes a threat and the few times it was needed she placed herself between her family and danger and stood her ground, barking, growling and showing a mouthful of big white teeth. Very intimidating indeed. I was babysitting a friend's infant one afternoon and chatting with Mickey when Luci sounded the alert.

The other dogs took a cue from her and began to bark savagely at our back fence. Luci raged up and down the fence in a highly agitated manner, which was unusual for her, and the other dogs joined in. It's private property back there, owned by a neighbor who let us graze our horses there. It's wooded and I wasn't able to see what they were so fired up about without disturbing the sleeping baby in my arms, but I commented to Mickey that it was unusual and she agreed. Her back had been bothering her so she didn't get up either and the commotion soon died away.

About fifteen minutes later Dave called from work to tell me he was listening to his dispatch radio and overheard a sheriff's department call of a sexual assault to a pregnant woman less than a quarter of a mile from us.

Deputies were searching for the suspect, who was last seen headed through the trees behind my house. Oh, my god! The dogs had just been going crazy right there. Without a doubt it was the suspect. I heard a helicopter circling overhead and a sheriff's car pulled into my driveway the moment I got off the phone with Dave. I went outside to speak to the deputy and gave him permission to search behind the house.

I found Nikki and Shay playing volleyball in the yard and asked them to come inside. Scott walked in about then and I told him about it. He was livid that someone would assault a woman. He offered to call in and ask to be excused from work to stay with us but I told him we would be okay. A few moments later I saw him on the phone with his employer anyway. For the next hour or so my muscular, six-foot-tall son played ball in the yard with Hula, the entire time scanning the surrounding areas. I could see how offended and angry he was. Scott has a very strong sense of right and wrong and hurting a pregnant woman neared the top of the "wrong" list.

It was night and pitch black when I remembered that I hadn't fed the horses yet. There's no light in my small barn, which is set away from the house, and backs right up the wooded area. I grabbed the flashlight and headed outside with the dogs who raced ahead and charged eagerly into the barn as the horses whinnied a greeting. My flashlight battery was dying and I had to feel my way around in the dark to find the alfalfa and toss it into the mangers. I had the heebie-jeebies thinking that if not for Luci and the other dogs the guy very well could have hidden out there. The cops were hot on his trail and there aren't many hiding places in the area. The next day I learned they had caught the guy hiding in a shed not a block from our home. I shuddered to think of it. My guess is the owners of that shed didn't have a Doberman.

As Luci and I spend time just being quiet together, I lie on her bed with her and tell her how much I love her, how special she is to us, how precious and wonderful. I breathe in her familiar odor, sweet and smoky from her bed in front of the fireplace. The occasional whiff of her breath, slightly ammonia smelling from her failing kidneys, is a bitter reminder of her condition. I stroke and massage her body. Her once muscular shoulders and thighs are wasted and her eyes look tired, but for a while she still wants to play when we walk down the driveway to get the paper in the morning. I hold her paws in my hands; her nails are getting a little long but they aren't affecting her walking so I'm not going to bother her with it.

She seems resigned to the pills and the needles lately. Luci was always a hearty eater but no longer. As her illness progresses, she eats less and less. She never would eat much of the special renal diet food that costs around a million dollars a pound. I researched alternative renal diets and started cooking chicken, rice and carrots for her and adding them to the kibble. For a while she ate that fairly well then pretty soon she ate all but the kibble, so I just gave her the cooked stuff. Then she started refusing the carrots and I started leaving those out. She eventually refused everything but the chicken, so I made her chicken with lots of broth. Finally, the day came when she couldn't even eat the chicken. She tried for me, and she wanted it, but she would only take a small piece from my hand and set it down, unable to eat.

I had been letting her do anything that made her happy. If I was going out and she wanted to go with me, I took her. Sometimes she was up to going along to work with me or going to the store, other times she wasn't; I let her decide. I bought her bully sticks, once her favorite treat, and she still wanted them but she no longer chewed on them, she just liked having them in bed with her.

I had planned a baby shower for a friend at my home on a Sunday and Luci was having a bad day. She hadn't eaten in a couple of days and rarely left her bed. I wished I could cancel the shower but I cuddled with her instead and my friends kindly decorated and prepared the food. The people there were some of my dearest friends, including my sister, and they all loved Luci. Everyone spent time with her, saying their good-byes and giving her attention. Luci had always loved company and usually spent the whole time going from person to person to rest her head on laps and cuddle. This time everyone visited around her bed and I could see she liked that.

I was off all day that Monday and I cancelled most of my plans and just hung out with her. I sat with her until she fell asleep then lay on the couch and read a book. I turned on the TV for the first time in about six months and lost myself in some mindless show while I absently stroked her legs. I did keep a lunch date with a friend as it was very nearby. As Luci grew weaker she had stopped wanting to go for a ride and hadn't asked to go for a week or so but that day she stood up as my friend and I left to go to lunch. I held the door for her and she walked slowly out to the car and waited for the door to open. Once inside, she settled on her blanket and watched the scenery out the window.

Since her terminal diagnosis months ago, I had dreaded what was coming. We had even tried an experimental stem cell transplant as one had been quite helpful with a serious illness she'd had years before. I have counseled hundreds of people on euthanasia. I always advise them to weigh quality of life: pain versus joy. Can the animal walk, do they still want to eat, are they continent most of the time? How much pain are they in? Can they still enjoy some of the things they liked before?

That day Luci still wanted to walk down to get the paper and she wanted to go for a ride, but she didn't eat at all and when we got home from lunch she went straight to bed for the rest of the day. She never even got up when I fed the other dogs. I brought her some chicken and she seemed to want it but wasn't able to eat it.

I tucked Luci in that night and lay down on the couch next to her feeling sad and sick to my stomach. I dozed, and she woke me up several times in the night to go out. Around 3:30 a.m. Luci woke me again to go outside. She'd had horrible diarrhea for the last few days but still would come and get me to let her out and then she would walk far into the orchard to go.

When she asked to be let in a few minutes later she looked absolutely haggard. She had lost so much weight and her eyes were weary. I tucked her into her bed and wrapped her blanket around her, but she couldn't seem to get warm or comfortable. I lay next to her, stroked her sweet face and listened to her breathing, waiting for her to fall asleep. She stared at me for the longest time, but finally put her head down and closed her eyes. Her breathing was ragged and her body felt tense. I put my face against her silky cheek and hugged her close as I came to terms with the fact there would be no miracles this time. I could not let my girl go on like this, weak, sick, in pain, wasting away to nothing and unable to eat. I dripped miserable tears on her face as I tried to decide if I should take her to the emergency room right away or wait until morning and have Dr. Patti come to the house to euthanize her. I wanted her to go in her own home, in her own bed, so I decided to try to keep her comfortable until morning. I gave her another dose of her pain medication and steeled myself for the morning.

I was trying to keep it together to avoid upsetting her, but when I went in the other room for a Kleenex I broke down and sobbed hard for a few minutes. Then I went back in and lay beside her in the dim light from the stained-glass lamp turned low. The house was quiet. Paul was in London for work, Mickey, the kids and the other animals were sound asleep. Everyone had been advised of her condition and the need to say good-bye. There was nothing left to do. It was just us, together for our last night. I pulled a blanket over us and wrapped my arms around her. Her breath was warm on my skin as I prayed for her to be relieved of her pain. I held her close as I thought back through our years together until, finally, we both slept.

I awoke with a start in the very early dawn and lay quietly in the darkness, not sure what had awakened me. Slowly, I realized the tension was gone from the still-warm body beside me. Sometime in the early morning hours, my girl had left me.

45. A Keeper

    With Luci gone, I tried to focus on my family, work and the other animals instead of being in a miserable funk all the time. I continued to work with Annie and she improved all the time. I gave Katie, the sweet old Borzoi, extra cuddles and massages. Katie's getting up there but she's still gorgeous, vigorous and happy. Little Rocky is old, too, but he's just the same as he's always been. He likes coming to work with me and I take him occasionally. I play ball with Hula and spend extra time brushing her beautiful golden coat. Tyra is still fostered with us and I listed her with Great Dane rescue as I continued to work with her. She was so scrawny and pathetic when she came to the shelter but now she's rippling with muscle and her shiny black coat is absolutely gorgeous. She makes Dobermans look like little pip-squeaks. We have actually had Danes and Saint Bernards turned into the shelter for getting

245

too big. It makes me crazy when that happens. It's not like it's a secret they get huge. What the heck are people thinking?

Each morning Tyra follows me out to the car to go to work. The continued socialization is critical for her to be a happy pet. She always has a toy in her mouth and she jumps in and settles down. At work she visits with staff and then lies down in Luci's old bed next to my desk. It gives me a pang to see her there and yet I know that caring for another rescue is a wonderful way to honor Luci. When we leave the shelter she puts her big feet up in the front seat of the truck and I boost her in. I put a cat carrier on the passenger side floor and then put blankets over it and laid a dog bed on top so it gives her a little more room to lie down. In spite of her size in the cab of the truck she's really good and curls up happily.

My sadness about losing Luci hangs over me and occasionally I break down and cry. She was such a good girl, so young, I think, as my tears fall and I bury my head in my hands, overcome with grief. Suddenly, a huge head shoves its way into my lap and an ecstatic Great Dane pushes her way in as close to me as she can get. I hug her thick neck and cry harder as she wiggles and wags and licks away my tears.

I have been looking for a rescued Doberman to adopt. No one will ever take Luci's place, of course, but I do love the affectionate and protective nature most Dobes have. I scan the rescue website every few days. Meanwhile, Tyra is as exuberantly happy as she once was depressed. I have to grin as she prances around with her toys sporting a huge, goofy grin on her face. My other animals love her because she's gentle and not pushy. The only problem is they go around with squinty eyes in an attempt to avoid her constantly lashing tail.

Tyra comes and buries her head in my lap as I surf the web for rescue Dobes. She sits next to me and stares into my face. "What is it, honey?" I ask. "Do you want to go out?" I get up and head for the door but she stays rooted in place, gazing at me eagerly. When I speak to her the tail whips harder. The bangs and thumps of her tail resonate through the house, as do the complaints of her tail-lashing victims. She still has a few deficits due to her lack of socialization as a puppy. She shrinks from some strangers, but overall Tyra is a happy girl. She has a toy in her mouth almost every waking moment and she wags and prances as she shows off her prize. We've had a few people express an interest in her but none of them were the right home for one reason or another. "Nobody wants a giant monster dog that eats like a horse and breaks things with her tail," I tease as she bounces around the house, clearing the coffee table in a single sweep.

In the truck she curls up on her bed and watches me drive. When I arrive on a call she sits up and checks out the action from the seat. If I'm having a stressful day she leans across the console and I stroke her head as I steady my breathing. Dogs are so amazing, I think, as look into her happy face. How can I stay miserable when Tyra's so dang happy?

I take another call from someone interested in Tyra. The guy wants a really big dog to protect his property. When I ask if she'll be allowed in the house, he hems and haws and says yeah, sometimes. That's code for never. "Don't worry, darling," I tell her as she shoves her head against me. "You're not going to be a junkyard dog."

We have a busy couple of weeks and I finally get a chance to check the Doberman rescue website again. They do such a great job, I think, as I skim the photos. Tyra and Chuck, our big orange cat, are cuddled up on the dog bed next to the computer as I peruse. I see a Dobe that looks good but as I read further I see that he's not good with cats. Oh well, the right dog will come along, I think, as I scroll down. At that moment Tyra gets up and comes over to shove her huge head against me, practically knocking me over. Her whole body is rocking back and forth and she gazes into my face with her silly doggie grin. "You are a giant monster dog," I tell her. "You almost knocked me out of my chair." But I have to laugh. She's adorable and she's overcome so much — lack of socialization, abandonment, trauma, kennel cough, mange — and her spirit has come through. I admire her ability to embrace the happy life she has now.

I stare at her for a moment and a thought that has been fluttering around in my mind for weeks takes rest in my consciousness. I still want another

Doberman someday, but with blinding clarity I realize what Tyra has been trying to tell me all along. Tyra is my dog and she's not going anywhere.

Acknowledgments

I offer my most heartfelt thank you to the following:

My incredibly loving and supportive husband, Paul Zindler. You are the love of my life, my dearest friend and have made all my prayers and dreams come true. Scott, Nikki and Shay for your love and patience when I head out to emergencies in the middle of meals, homework, birthdays, holidays and special days. Being a mother is one of the great joys of my life and I love you more than words can say. My mom for instilling in me a love of animals and indulging my need to rescue every creature I came across from the moment I was old enough to walk. My father for letting me tag along on horseback all day as a child. Mickey for holding down the fort and doing the doggie juggle for me when I'm stuck on late calls. My terrific family and friends who have encouraged and believed in me. Doug and Patti Sloan, my dear and precious friends who helped make it all happen. Dr. Grant Miller, Katie Moore, and everyone at the Sonoma CHANGE Program for making a huge difference to the horses in our community. Steve and Jennie Sisler for adopting my foster girl, Daisy, and supporting the book project in a big way. Bad Rap for tirelessly advocating for our current most misunderstood breed. My fellow animal control officers, shelter workers and rescuers who make a difference every day. And to my editor, Suzanne Sherman, for endless support and assistance.

Made in the USA
Lexington, KY
26 April 2017